ORIGINS

A GUIDE TO THE PLACE NAMES OF GRAND TETON NATIONAL PARK

AND THE SURROUNDING AREA

Initial research and text by Elizabeth Wied Hayden
Revised and written by Cynthia Nielsen

Additional contributions and editing by
Friends and Staff of Grand Teton National Park

Project coordination by Sharlene Milligan
Use of maps courtesy of Bill Resor
Unless otherwise identified, the photographs are the property of
The National Park Service
Design by Riddell Advertising & Design
Lithography by Lorraine Press

Cover art extracted from the Map of The Sources of the Snake River
from the Sixth Annual Report of the United States Geological Survey
of the Territories by Ferdinand V. Hayden, 1873

TABLE OF CONTENTS

How To Get The Most From This Book

THE BODY OF THIS BOOK, BEGINNING ON PAGE 12, IS AN alphabetical listing of the place names of Grand Teton National Park and the Jackson Hole area. The information following each reference is intended to be concise. For more information on the history of Jackson Hole, refer to one of the many excellent available histories such as *From Trapper to Tourist*, the Grand Teton Natural History Association's companion to this book.

A number of local names are not included because information on the background, source, or date of naming is lacking. Therefore, the publisher of this book encourages contributions about area place names. Send information, including the address or location of each verifiable source, to:

Place Names Coordinator
Grand Teton Natural History Association
Post Office Box 170
Moose, Wyoming 83012

Place names are listed alphabetically. Names commonly preceded by an article such as "a," "an," or "the," are alphabetized by the second word in the name. Names of mountain peaks beginning with "Mount" are alphabetized by the second word in the name. For example, Mount Owen is placed under O, not under M.

Some alphabetical entries include an abbreviation, such as GLO, USGS, USGB, and the date the feature was officially named or mapped. An explanation of these five abbreviations follows:

GLO — a reference to the *General Land Office Maps of Wyoming*.

YTLR — a reference to the *Yellowstone Timber Land Reserve Map of 1899*.

FS — an abbreviation of the *Teton National Forest Map of 1912*.

USGS — a reference to a map compiled by the *United States Geologic Survey*.

USGB — *Decisions of the U.S. Geographic Board* report.

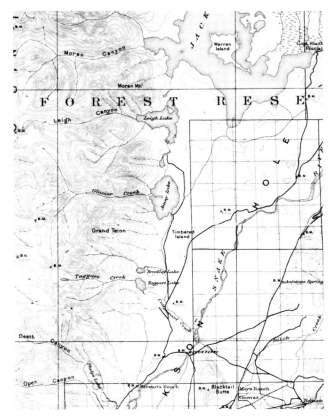

EXTRACT OF U.S. GEOLOGICAL SURVEY MAP, EDITION OF APRIL 1901

Some of the most colorful names date prior to the 1900s. The Hayden surveys of 1872 and 1878, as well as T.M. Bannon's survey conducted in the summers of 1898 and 1899, named many features. In some cases these expeditions merely recorded names already in use. They also bestowed many names of their own creation. For a more thorough understanding of their role in Jackson Hole's place name history, please continue through the next section entitled "What's in a Name?"

WHAT'S IN A NAME?

FOR TEN THOUSAND YEARS BANDS OF INDIANS PASSED through the valleys on both sides of the Teton Range. Here camped the mountain men and trappers, and, on the west side of the Teton Range, they held rendezvous. Settlers came to build new lives and communities. In this place memories and history do not fade away, but seem to echo endlessly, and arise at the slightest beckoning, to catch the imagination and quicken the pulse.

Much of the area's history is stored in the names of its places and landmarks. The people who gave names to the places sometimes were striving to do more than merely label. They tried to give lasting identity to that particular mountain, stream, meadow, or alpine lake that inspired them beyond the labels—beyond the questions of how high? how deep? or how old?

Places and people are named for many of the same reasons: after a person, to commemorate an event, because of a distinguishing physical characteristic, or often simply to differentiate between one and another. Sometimes those responsible for the naming were successful in capturing the aura or significance of a place. Sometimes they were not. Place names run the complete scale from the inappropriate, to the historical, to the poetic. Consider these examples: Mount Meek. Grand, imposing, awesome maybe; but not meek. Mount Meek could sound wrong as a name for this mountain on the southern rim of Alaska Basin, but it could have been worse. Imagine, "Meek Peak."

Or consider Jackson Hole. The term "hole" was used by early explorers to mean an upper elevation valley nearly surrounded by mountains. The "Jackson" was David E. Jackson, a beaver trapper, after whom the hole was named, probably in 1829, by his partner Bill Sublette because Jackson considered it his favorite trapping ground. Originally called Jackson's Hole, the name gradually changed in modern usage owing to ease of pronunciation and the indelicate jokes associated with the original name.

Place names of Jackson Hole and the Teton Range do not all derive from historical interest. Men were often moved to reach for poetry to describe the beauty that they encountered. As the name Columbine Cascades rolls off the tongue, the mind conjures up an image of a special place. Seen from a distance, Columbine Cascades does not plunge over the edge of a cliff as do so many waterfalls. Instead it lies like a watery veil across terraced rock. Picture the rippling water bordered by columbine—colored-flowers that look more like scattered bouquets than rooted plants—and you will understand that no other name is better for this remote backcountry cascade. Names can also illuminate the natural history of Jackson Hole. The ouzel is a gray bird about the size of a robin. It dives under the rushing water and walks along the stream bottom to feed on aquatic insects. It often builds its nest and raises its young behind the protection of an overhanging waterfall. When one possesses this information, the name Ouzel Falls becomes appropriate.

THE HUMAN IMPRINT ON AREA PLACE NAMES

BEGINNING WITH THE AREA'S EARLIEST INHABITANTS, THIS historical survey will examine place name sources—Indian tribes, fur trappers, soldiers, and surveyors—who have left the stamp of their identities on Jackson Hole.

INDIANS AND TRAPPERS

CURRENT RESEARCH SHOWS THAT AS EARLY AS 10,000, YEARS ago, Indians were migrating into and out of Jackson Hole. There were two culturally separate and distinct groups which used two routes to enter and leave the Jackson Hole area. One route led from the Green River Basin, along Bacon Ridge, and down the Gros Ventre River. The other came from what is now Yellowstone National Park, headed toward the northern end of Jackson Lake and then went out over Conant Pass to Idaho. Later these trails were used by fur trappers and settlers as routes into Jackson Hole, but modern roads do not utilize either of these ancient gateways.

Archeological evidence supports the theory that no Indians occupied Jackson Hole on a permanent basis. In the summer, Indians came to hunt buffalo, and made camps near Blacktail Butte and on what is now the National Elk Refuge. Early Indians came into the valley from different regions to fish, to gather camas bulbs that grew in the meadows, and to set up temporary camps on the northern end of Jackson Lake. By late summer these people were moving into the high country to hunt bighorn sheep.

Beginning about 1800 the Indian tribes that frequented Jackson Hole can be identified. All of these tribes possessed horses by 1800 and were more mobile than ever before. Jackson Hole lay on the northeastern edge of hunting grounds claimed by the Snake Indians. The Gros Ventre, Flathead, and Blackfoot traveled through Jackson Hole either enroute to fur trade rendezvous or on their way to raid the Shoshoni, their traditional enemies. Togwotee, John Enos, and Tosi—Shoshonis who guided for hunters and explorers in this region during the 1800s—left their names on the topography.

Either because groups of Indians passed through Jackson Hole on summer forays, or simply because it lay between them and their destination, none claimed it as territory. The most frequent Indian visitors to Jackson Hole were small bands of secretive Sheepeater Indians of the Shoshoni stock. Unlike most tribes of the time, they lacked horses and were very wary of the trappers who were beginning to infiltrate the area. Shoshoko has been translated to mean "walker" in the Shoshoni language, and is probably a reference to the horseless Sheepeater.

Names for other features in the area come from Indian words as translated by early fur trappers and explorers. The name of the Yellowstone River was first recorded by Lewis and Clark, who were merely translating the French fur trappers' name for the river, Roche Juane, Yellow Rock River. In turn, the trappers were believed to be translating the Indian name which had described the yellow color of the rocks in the Grand Canyon of the Yellowstone River.

The Yellowstone, Snake, Gros Ventre, and the Wind rivers were important to early travelers for two reasons. First, the river drainages offered natural routes into this mountain valley ringed by high peaks. Second, trappers preferred the river routes because there they would find beaver. These waterways, too rough to be navigated, were some of the earliest named features in the Jackson Hole region.

The Snake River, with its long and twisted course to the Columbia, has a lengthy history of mapping and naming. On Williams Clark's map of 1810 it was called the Lewis River or Lewis Fork, in honor of Clark's partner Merriwether Lewis. Trappers in the Rocky Mountain West largely ignored this name. They referred to the Snake as the Mad River.

In 1811, Wilson Price Hunt led the first overland party to the Pacific Ocean since Lewis and Clark. Known as the Astorians, the expedition was employed by John Jacob Astor and his American Fur Company. The earliest references to the upper Snake River as the Mad River appeared in Washington Irving's account of that expedition. The river did not appear officially as the Snake River until 1840. Captain Benjamin L.E. Bonneville, an army captain on leave, led an expedition west in 1832. Funded by New York capitalists, Bonneville hoped to gather geographical information and explore the commercial opportunities in the West. Bonneville's map of 1837 shows the Snake River on the west side of the Teton Range. While Bonneville's map shows the Three Tetons, "Jackson's Big Hole," and "Jackson's Little Hole" (on the Hoback River), it completely omits Jackson Lake and the upper Snake River. Early mappers depended upon trappers' vague verbal accounts and descriptions of the area, and inaccuracies were bound to appear.

Possibly the first whiteman to visit Jackson Hole was John Colter. Colter first came west with the Lewis and Clark Expedition in 1804. He wanted to remain behind to trap furs on the Yellowstone and upper Missouri rivers, and was released from the Lewis and Clark Expedition in 1806. Colter then met and joined the Manuel Lisa fur trading party out of St. Louis. Because Colter was familiar with the area, Lisa sent him out to make contact with the Indians and pursuade them to trade at Lisa's new fort at the mouth of the Bighorn River. As Colter sought to achieve this, he probably entered Jackson Hole late in 1807, and possibly wintered in Pierre's Hole, on the west side of the Teton Range before returning to the fort via what is now Yellowstone National Park. Evidence of Colter's entrance into this valley lies with Clark's map published in 1814, which shows Colter's Route of 1807. The map places Colter at Lake Biddle (Clark's name for Jackson Lake) and at Lake Eustis (Yellowstone Lake), but it contains so many discrepancies that the exact route is unclear.

John Colter was one of many white men to enter Jackson Hole seeking furs. Beaver pelts lured the trappers who would follow. Major Andrew Henry led a trapping expedition out from Lisa's Fort on the Bighorn River to the Three Forks on the Missouri River. After being plagued by Blackfoot Indians, Henry's group crossed the Continental Divide at Targhee Pass and built a group of cabins along a tributary of the Snake River that came to be called Henry's Fork. A hunter from Kentucky, John Hoback, was with Henry's party. In the spring of 1811, Hoback, Jacob Reznor and Edward Robinson left Henry's "Fort," as it was called, crossed Teton Pass from the west into Jackson Hole, and left by way of Togwotee Pass. As the three men traveled down the Missouri River, they met the overland Astorians led by Wilson Price Hunt. Hunt persuaded the Hoback party to join his expedition as guides. In the fall of 1811 Hunt's Astorians, guided by Hoback and his two companions, first viewed the Tetons from the vicinity of Union Pass. The guides hailed the peaks as familiar landmarks from their trapping ventures the year before. Hunt later referred to the Tetons as "Pilot Knobs" because of their elevation above the surrounding plain. They served as landmarks for the Astorians' route to the mouth of the Columbia River. Hunt and his party entered Jackson Hole via a major tributary of the Snake River which Hunt named the Hoback River to honor his guide.

Wilson Price Hunt also named a river on the eastern margin of Jackson Hole country. During the 1811 expedition, the Astorians followed a stream that Hunt described as a branch of the Bighorn River. They called it the Wind River because,

as Hunt informed Washington Irving, ". . . this blast . . . said to be caused by a narrow gap or funnel in the mountains . . ." blows so continuously in winter that snow will not accumulate along its banks.

The Gros Ventre River, the other major stream in the area, was no doubt named by French-speaking fur trappers passing through Jackson Hole sometime in the early 1800s. In French, Gros Ventre (pronounced Grow Vaunt) means "big belly." The Gros Ventre Indians, also known as the Atsinas, had long used this stream as a pathway to travel from Montana to visit their Arapahoe relatives living along the South Platte River. The Gros Ventre evidently crossed into Jackson Hole to avoid the Crows. The name first appears on W.A. Ferris' map of 1836, spelled "Grosvent Fork."

On July 18, 1832, as the annual Pierre's Hole rendezvous drew to its boisterous conclusion, a party of trappers led by Milton Sublette departed. Nathaniel Wyeth's group, some smaller parties, and a group of free trappers banded together and accompanied Sublette to insure safe passage. As they ascended Teton Pass from the west, they were attacked by Gros Ventre Indians. William Sublette, Milton's brother, had gotten word of the attack while he was still at the rendezvous and hurried in with reinforcements. In the battle, William Sublette was shot in the arm. Five whites and seven Indian allies lost their lives. More than twenty Gros Ventre Indians were reported killed. The trappers buried their dead and returned to rendezvous for a few days to recover.

On July 25, a week after the battle, eight trappers, too anxious to leave to wait for the Sublette party, started out alone. As they passed through Jackson Hole near the mouth of the Hoback River, they were ambushed. Two trappers, George More of Boston and a Mr. Foy from Mississippi, were killed, and the leader of the group received a wound that proved fatal.

Warren Ferris, a clerk for the American Fur Company, passed through Jackson Hole in August of 1832, and in his journal entry of August 14 he described his discovery of the remains of More and Foy:

JOSEPH MEEK TRAPPED IN JACKSON HOLE

DURING THE HEIGHT OF THE FUR TRADE, 1830-1840.

THE EMBROIDERY ON THE POSSIBLES BAG AT

HIS WAIST IS OF INDIAN ORIGIN.

ORIGINAL PHOTO BY JOS. BUCKTEL, ENGRAVING BY J.C. BUTTRE.

On the 14th we passed through the Narrows, between Jackson's Holes; and avoided some of the difficulties we met with on our previous passage by crossing the river several times. In the evening we halted for the night near the remains of two men who were killed in July last. These we collected, and deposited in a small stream that discharged itself into a fork of the Lewis River, that flows from Jackson's Little Hole.

An 1837 map made by Warren Ferris for his employees was the first to show Jackson Hole by name, but it was not published until after 1900. Captain Bonneville's map of 1837 is better known, but less accurate than the map made by Ferris. Both men showed the Three Tetons, but Bonneville omitted Jackson Lake and the section of the Snake River within Jackson Hole, Ferris included Jackson Lake, which he called Teton Lake.

Reverend Samuel Parker's map of 1838 was the first to map three buttes (now known as Blacktail, East Gros Ventre, and West Gros Ventre buttes) in Jackson Hole. In his "Journal of an Exploring Tour," published in 1842, Parker was the first to include the location of Stinking Springs in southern Jackson Hole. He called them simply "sulphur springs."

In 1826 Davey Jackson, William Sublette, and Jedediah Smith formed a partnership and bought the Rocky Mountain Fur Company from General William Ashley and Major Andrew Henry. Jackson remains the most obscure of this group. His signature appears on company documents, but he kept no journal. It seems that he was well liked and well known among the fur trappers of the Rocky Mountain area, but little is known of his life before he joined the Rocky Mountain Fur Company. Evidently, he spent the winter of 1828-29 in the vicinity of Jackson Hole and had met Sublette on the shores of Jackson Lake following the Wind River rendezvous in the summer of that year. In 1830, Jackson, Smith, and William Sublette sold their company interests to his brother Milton Sublette, Thomas Fitzpatrick, Jim Bridger, Henry Fraeb and Baptiste Gervais. After the sale of the company, the original partners separated. Davey Jackson left the Rockies for California. Jedediah Smith was killed by Indians on the Santa Fe Trail in 1831. William Sublette returned to the Rockies for the 1832 rendezvous in Pierre's Hole.

On the Green River in 1840, the last fur trade rendezvous was held. Beaver felt top hats had been replaced by silk hats, and cutthroat competition between the American Fur Company and the Rocky Mountain Fur Company had exhausted the beaver supply. It was the end of an era.

SOLDIERS AND SURVEYORS

THE ERA OF THE FUR TRAPPER AND MOUNTAIN MAN WAS over, but Jackson Hole was not forgotten. Hunters and solitary trappers continued to frequent the area. The federal government funded numerous military and civilian survey expeditions to obtain more reliable information on the West.

In 1860, Captain William F. Raynolds, of the Army's Topographical Engineers, led an expedition into Jackson Hole. Guided by Jim Bridger, well known explorer, the expedition sought more complete information concerning the region of the upper Yellowstone, Gallatin, and Madison rivers. Of particular interest was the potential for railroad routes.

The expedition crossed the Wind River Range via Union Pass (named by Raynolds) and followed the Gros Ventre River into Jackson Hole. After following the Snake River south, the party turned westward and crossed Teton Pass. On the pass they discovered a tree with the inscription "J M July 7 1832   July 11 1833." Joe Meek may have carved the inscription.

A geologist named Ferdinand Vandiver Hayden accompanied Raynolds. In the 1870s, Hayden led numerous U.S. Geological Survey expeditions into the Rocky Mountain West. These surveys proved significant in mapping, surveying, and naming topographical features in Jackson Hole. Dr. Hayden headed the Yellowstone and Snake River surveys in 1872. His geologist, Frank H. Bradley, commanded the Snake River Division of the survey. As they entered Jackson Hole from the Yellowstone country, they were guided through the valley by an itinerant hunter and trapper named Beaver Dick Leigh. This 1872 expedition left its mark on Jackson Hole in the form of many new place names. Two members of the group, James Stevenson,

PHOTOGRAPHER WILLIAM H. JACKSON ACCOMPANIED

THE HAYDEN EXPEDITIONS IN 1872 AND 1878. ALTHOUGH JACKSON TOOK

THE FIRST PHOTOS OF THE TETON RANGE FROM TABLE MOUNTAIN

ON THE WEST SIDE OF THE RANGE, HE IS NOT THE "JACKSON" FOR

WHICH THE VALLEY IS NAMED. JACKSON HOLE WAS NAMED FOR

FUR TRAPPER DAVID JACKSON.

TETON COUNTY LIBRARY BICENTENNIAL PHOTO COLLECTION.

leader of the Snake River division, and N.P. Langford, who became the first superintendent of Yellowstone National Park, attempted to climb the Grand Teton. Their difficult ascent from the west was the first recorded attempt on the Grand Teton. They claimed to have reached the summit but left no evidence there.

Two glacial lakes at the eastern foot of the Teton Range were named for Bradley and his assistant, Rush Taggart. Leigh Lake honored their guide, Beaver Dick Leigh and Jenny Lake was named after his Shoshoni wife. They named Coulter Creek, a tributary of the upper Yellowstone River, for John M. Coulter the expedition's botanist, and Mount Leidy in honor of their paleontologist Joseph Leidy. Dr. Hayden named Mount Moran for Thomas Moran, the artist who accompanied the Yellowstone portion of the expedition and painted landscapes that influenced Congress to set aside Yellowstone as the world's first national park.

The 1872 expedition also recorded the names of Teton Pass, Buffalo Fork, and Teton Creek (which is now named Cascade Creek), on their maps. Bradley's report, which appears in Hayden's Sixth Annual Report, also named the Grand Teton "Mount Hayden" to honor the leader of the expedition. Hayden did not favor the name and insisted that Grand Teton be used.

In 1877 Hayden's expedition sent another party into Jackson Hole under the leadership of G.B. Bechler. Orestes St. John, a geologist, accompanied him and wrote the report of their survey, published in Hayden's Eleventh Annual Report. In 1931, Mount St. John was named to commemorate him. Pacific Creek, Blackrock Creek, Mount Baird, Phelps Lake, Togwotee Pass were additions not previously shown on the 1872 survey maps. Phelps Lake was named for a trapper, George Phelps, who reported the presence of the lake to the expedition. Many old-time residents feel that Phillips Canyon, near Phelps Lake, was named after the same trapper, but that the spelling was corrupted.

Captain W.A. Jones named Togwotee Pass several years before the 1877 Hayden expedition in honor of his Shoshoni Indian guide. Jones was exploring the feasibility of a new route through Yellowstone for the U.S. Army. He entered Yellowstone from the east and then departed via Two Ocean Pass and Togwotee Pass. Captain Jones verified the existence of Two Ocean Pass on the Continental Divide.

William O. Owen surveyed Jackson Hole in 1892, although he is more often remembered as a mountain climber than as a surveyor. Along with John Shive, Frank Petersen, and Bishop Franklin Spalding, Owen climbed the Grand Teton in August of 1898. The Wyoming Legislature credited them with the first ascent. Mount Owen was named for him in 1927.

The U.S. Geological Survey made the first standard topographical map of the Teton Range in 1899. Under the direction of T.M. Bannon, this survey produced the Grand Teton and Mount Leidy quadrangles. Interest in the timber reserves here and in Yellowstone provided the impetus for the survey. Bannon, assisted by E.M. Douglas, Frank Tweedy, Arthur Stiles, and G.E. Hyde, added several important place names to the maps—Granite, Open, Death, Leigh, and Moran canyons. Buck Mountain, which does not appear on a map until 1924, also dates back to this period. Bannon called the triangulation station established on the summit of this mountain, Buck Station, after George Buck, his recorder. The name of Blacktail Butte was formally established by Bannon's 1899 map. Early maps referred to this butte as North Gros Ventre Butte or simply Gros Ventre Butte.

The last chapter of the history behind the place names found in Jackson Hole is not yet complete. It began with the establishment of Grand Teton National Park in 1929. When the Park was created, many natural features were unnamed. Among the ranger staff that first summer of operation were two men who had climbed extensively in the Teton Range since 1926. Fritiof Fryxell, the Park's first ranger naturalist, and Phil Smith, a homesteader turned ranger, are credited with many first acsents of Teton peaks. To help identify peaks in conversation and correspondence, Fryxell and Smith began to name the peaks they climbed. In 1930 Superintendent Sam Woodring requested that Fryxell submit his recommended names for geographic features. These were included in a list

THIS BIRD'S-EYE VIEW OF JACKSON WAS PHOTOGRAPHED

IN THE EARLY 1920s ACCORDING TO MRS. VILATE SEATON MORRIS,

AN EARLY AND LIFELONG RESIDENT OF THE VALLEY.

IT WAS ORIGINALLY INTENDED FOR USE AS A POSTCARD.

TETON COUNTY LIBRARY BICENTENNIAL PHOTO COLLECTION.

of names sent for appraisal to the United States Board on Geographic Names. They were approved in 1931. In a letter written several years later, Fryxell described his feelings toward the naming of these peaks:

> *Though at first intended for our own use we chose these names thoughtfully, I might even say lovingly, for to us every peak had come to possess its own distinctive personality . . . we were both surprised and pleased to note how quickly many of them were adopted.*

One needs to simply open a Park map and names like Colter, Leigh, and Jackson provide instant recognition of times gone by. Davey Jackson would certainly have been amazed by the millions of people who visit Jackson Hole, and perhaps he would be pleased at the many place names that reflect the history and appreciation of this special place.

Index To Place Names

ADAMS CANYON   Runs into Mosquito Creek from the south. Named for early settlers, brothers Brig and Josh Adams.

ALASKA BASIN   Just outside the western boundary of Grand Teton National Park. Probably named by early settlers who went to Alaska during the gold rush.

ALKALI CREEK   Flows from the south into the Gros Ventre River, above Lower Slide Lake. Its waters contain sodium sulfate, bitter-tasting minerals from the adjoining lime-colored hills which are part of the Gros Ventre Mountains.

AMPHITHEATER LAKE   A small lake in the Teton Range between Glacier Gulch and Garnet Canyon. Set in an amphitheater-like glacial cirque which encompasses the lake on three sides. USGB Map 1931.

ANGLE MOUNTAIN (el. 10,566')   Just east of Togwotee Lodge. Named for Albert A. Angle, who built the old Togwotee Lodge in the 1920's.

ANTELOPE FLATS   North of Blacktail Butte. Antelope migrate into Jackson Hole for the summer and can often be seen browsing on these flats. USGB Map 1908.

ANTELOPE PASS   A mile west of Jackson, Highway 26 makes a right-angle turn to the south. Now simply called "The Y." During the early years of settlement, hundreds of antelope migrated from the south, many through this pass.

ANTELOPE SPRING   Located on a timbered slope on the western side of Shadow Mountain. The spring was named for the flats.

APRES VOUS PEAK (el. 8,426')   Towers above Teton Village. From the French meaning "after you," named after the ski area was established in 1965.

ARIZONA CREEK   Runs into the northeastern corner of Jackson Lake. Named for Arizona George, who trapped in this area with his partner, Dog-faced Pete, in 1888. Arizona George was found dead on this creek.

ARIZONA ISLAND   Located on the northeastern side of Jackson Lake near the mouth of Arizona Creek. Originally a peninsula, it became an island when Jackson Lake was

Trail Construction Camp

of The Civilian Conservation Corps (CCC)

in Alaska Basin during the summer of 1931.

dammed. Named for Arizona George *(see Arizona Creek).*

ARIZONA LAKE   East of Jackson Lake. Named for Arizona George *(see Arizona Creek).*

ARIZONA PEAK   (el. 7,853') Between Arizona and Lizard creeks, northeast of Jackson Lake. Named for Arizona George *(see Arizona Creek).*

ARROWHEAD POOL   Easternmost of three alpine lakes in Hanging Canyon. Its outline suggests a flint arrowhead. USGB Map, 1931.

ASTORIA HOT SPRINGS   On the Snake River below Hoback Junction. Named for John Jacob Astor, founder of the American Fur Company in 1808. The springs were first owned by early settler George Bohnet, an Alsation, who had placer mined the hot springs and is said to have been the only successful miner. Later owned by Johnny Counts and called Counts' Hot Springs by early settlers.

ATHERTON CREEK   A Gros Ventre River tributary that flows into Lower Slide Lake. Named for an early squatter, the only person living on the creek, who found the population along the Gros Ventre "to darned numerous." He moved his cabin some miles further into the hills in 1893.

ATLANTIC CREEK   In the Teton Wilderness. Atlantic Creek runs northeast from Two Ocean Pass into the upper Yellowstone River. Pacific and Atlantic creeks have the same source. Jim Bridger told Capt. W.F. Raynolds in 1860 that a stream of considerable size flows down either side of the watershed, discharging its waters into both the Atlantic and Pacific oceans. Shown on the GLO Map of 1876 and on Raynolds' 1859-60 Map as Two Ocean Creek.

AVALANCHE CANYON   Drained by Taggart Creek. Located in the Teton Range between Death and Garnet canyons. Avalanches occur frequently here, especially in spring. USGB Map, 1931.

BACON CREEK   Flows from the southeast into the Gros Ventre River. Settlers entered Jackson Hole along an age-old Indian trail that followed the creek. GLO plots for 1893 and Mount Leidy Quad, 1899. Creek named for ridge.

BACON RIDGE   Runs southeast from Bacon Creek. The ridge resembles a slab of bacon.

BAILEY CREEK   A small creek that runs into Arizona Creek, east of Jackson Lake. Named for Richard H. Bailey who homesteaded on the creek around 1915, and tried to winter cattle. Bailey's place was called both Bailey and Arizona meadows.

BALDY KNOLL   (el. 9,034') West of Marion Lake, outside the park. Its lack of vegetation give an impression of baldness.

BALDY MOUNTAIN   Northeast of Mt. Leidy. A feature of the knoll and mountain is the lack of vegetation and the impression of baldness.

BANNOCK FALLS   Located in Garnet Canyon. Named for the Bannock Indians who came from the west and frequented Jackson Hole before settlement. It was earlier called Bradley Canyon Falls.

BANNON, MOUNT   (el. 10,960') South of Mount Meek at the head of Death Canyon, between Buck and Fossil mountains. Named for T.M. Bannon, topographer, who established a triangulation station on Buck Mountain in 1898.

BASELINE FLAT   Between Timbered Island and the Snake River, opposite Antelope Flats. Named during the survey of Grand Teton National Park, a baseline was used in triangulation to determine the elevation and location of specific peaks. A "baseline" is a distance between two points on a map with a known length and position.

BATTLE MOUNTAIN   (el. 7,017') North of Hoback Canyon just beyond the mouth of Granite Creek. Named for a hunting disagreement in 1895 between Bannock Indians from Fort Hall, Idaho and early settlers. According to the Fort Bridger treaty of 1868, Indians were permitted to hunt on unoccupied land regardless of season. Wyoming had become a state in 1890 and had set a fall hunting season. It irked settlers that Indians could hunt in summer when they could not. A posse arrested a hunting party of Bannocks camped at what is now called Battle Mountain, and a minor battle resulted. Two Bannocks were shot, one fatally. A child was captured from the Indians, but later returned.

BATTLESHIP MOUNTAIN   (el. 10,079') Located north of Alaska

Basin on the west side of the Teton Range, just outside the Park. The east facing side resembles a battleship.

BEARD MOUNTAIN (el. 9,466′) Northwest of Lake Solitude on the western side of the Teton Range, outside the Park. The mountain was named for William Beard, an early resident.

BEAVER CREEK From its source on the eastern slope of Buck Mountain, Beaver Creek flows into Cottonwood Creek from the west. Beavers work and live along the creek at the base of the range. Nearby park employee housing and office area is also called Beaver Creek.

BERRY CREEK In the Teton Range in the northwestern corner of the Park. Named for A.J. Berry, living at the mouth of the creek at the turn of the century. Shown on Grand Teton Quad., for 1899.

BIERER CREEK Drains into Lower Slide Lake from the south. Named for old-timer Billie Bierer, well known for predicting the Gros Ventre slide of 1925.

BIG GAME RIDGE Extends southward from Yellowstone National Park into the Teton Wilderness within the Bridger-Teton National Forest. Called Elk Ridge in Raynolds' Report of 1859-60, and named by the USGS in 1885. One of the major summering grounds for the Jackson Hole elk herd.

BIVOUAC PEAK (el. 10,825′) Located in the Teton Range north of Mount Moran. First ascent was made on July 12, 1930, by a renowned party of mountaineers, Fritiof Fryxell, Theodore Koven and Gustav Koven. They named the peak after they were compelled to spend the night at the foot of the mountain without food or bedding.

BLACK CANYON Southeast of Teton Pass. Possibly named because of its heavy timber which is sometimes referred to as "black."

BLACKTAIL BUTTE (el. 7,688′) Located in the middle of Jackson Hole. First called Gros Ventre Butte by Doane in 1876. Presidential Proclamation map of 1904 shows it as Upper Gros Ventre Butte. Called Blacktail Butte on a 1899 survey map. Named for the blacktail deer, now commonly called mule deer, that graze the butte's slopes and upper meadows.

BLACKTAIL PONDS On the Snake River, north of Moose Village, near Blacktail Butte. Probably named for the butte.

BLUE MINER LAKE South of the Gros Ventre River, east of Sheep Mountain. Named for Bill Miner, a carpenter in Jackson before 1929.

BOBCAT RIDGE In the Teton Wilderness. Named because of occasional sightings of bobcats.

BOHNETT'S CANYON Runs into the Snake River from the southwest off of Munger Mountain at the south end of Jackson Hole. Named for George Bohnett, who settled in the valley in the early part of the century (see also Astoria Hot Springs).

BONNEY'S PINNACLE (el. 12,000′) The higher of the two pinnacles at the base of the northern ridge of the Middle Teton. Named for Orrin H. Bonney, author of "Bonney's Guide." First ascent on August 11, 1948, by Orrin and Rodger Bonney.

BOONE CREEK This creek and its accompanying ridge were named before 1870 for Robert Withrow, an eccentric pioneer of Irish descent who called himself "Daniel Boone, the Second."

BOTCHER HILL A one-half-mile incline, four miles north of Jackson, named for Henry Botcher, an influential citizen of Jackson Hole during the early 1900s. The major highway into Grand Teton National Park ascends this hill just before entering the southern Park boundary.

BOULDER ISLAND A small island at the southern end of Leigh Lake made by a huge boulder now partly covered by trees.

BOYLE'S HILL (el. 6,623′) South of West Gros Ventre Butte. Named for rancher James (Jim) Boyle, who owned the land and who tried in 1917 to travel to Jackson in a new Maxwell car. Unfortunately, the Snake River bridge had washed out, so he had to leave the car in Driggs.

BOX CREEK Runs out of a box canyon into the Buffalo Fork River near Turpin Meadows. Serves as a trailhead into the Teton Wilderness. Shown on the USGS Map of 1908.

BRADLEY LAKE At the base of the Teton Range. Drains into Cottonwood Creek, south of Jenny Lake. Named by F.V. Hayden for Frank H. Bradley, chief geologist of Hayden's 1872 expedition. Shown on maps and reports in the Geological and Geographical Surveys of the Territories, 1878.

BRECCIA PEAK (el. 11,010′) Just north of Togwotee Pass.

Primary composition is breccia, a type of conglomerate volcanic rock formed when broken rocks and pebbles are cemented together by molten lava.

BRIDGER LAKE   In the Teton Wilderness, just outside the south boundary of Yellowstone, close to the old trapper trails. Named by fur trappers for Jim Bridger, trapper and guide, who frequented this area for more than forty years, beginning in 1823. Shown on the Military Department of the Platte Map for 1874.

BROKEN FALLS   Located on an unnamed creek about a mile southwest of Jenny Lake, on the eastern flank of Teewinot Mountain. Named for its tumbling, broken cascades.

BROOKS LAKE   Situated east of Togwotee Pass. Named in 1904 for Bryant B. Brooks, who was then governor of Wyoming.

BROWN'S MEADOWS   Near the headwaters of Arizona Creek. Brown was an early trapper found frozen to death in the winter of 1898 by John Shive. Shive carved a gravestone for him, later replaced by a new stone carved by longtime resident Slim Lawrence in the 1940s.

BUCK MOUNTAIN (el. 11,938′)   Named for George A. Buck, recorder for T.M. Bannon's 1898 mapping party. Bannon gave the name "Buck Station" to the triangulation station he and George Buck established on the summit in 1898. Fritiof Fryxell, the first ranger naturalist in Grand Teton, thought Buck Mountain a rather prosaic name for one of his favorite peaks and suggested "Mt. Alpenglow," but the original was retained.

BURNED RIDGE   Glacial moraine, across from North Jenny Lake Junction, named by the Park Service in 1931 following an extensive study that revealed lightning-caused fires burned the ridge in 1765, 1856, 1879 and 1890. The moraine is an accumulation of boulders, stones, and debris carried and deposited by an enormous glacier.

BURNED WAGON GULCH   Located west of Timbered Island near the mouth of Garnet Canyon. In 1911, W.H. Saebohm, a Jackson Hole game warden, found a burned wagon and camp outfit in the gulch. Investigation revealed that a man named Reed and a man named Arnett had left Butte, Montana, with a similar wagon and camp outfit. Arnett had disappeared

THIS LIKENESS OF JIM BRIDGER,

FAMOUS FUR TRAPPER AND GUIDE,

IS TAKEN FROM THE ONLY

KNOWN PORTRAIT OF HIM, CIRCA 1866.

and was presumed murdered by Reed. Saebohm later found that a man named Reed was serving time in the Wyoming penitentiary for the murder of two brothers named Winslow.

BURNT CREEK A tributary of the Gros Ventre River south of Upper Slide Lake. Shown on the Mount Leidy Quad, 1899 *(see Burnt Point)*.

BURNT MOUNTAIN (el. 9,899') Between Bacon Creek and the south fork of the Gros Ventre River *(see Burnt Point)*.

BURNT POINT (el. 9,983') West of Crystal Creek in the Gros Ventre Range. Extensive lightning caused fires burned in this area during 1765, 1856, 1879, and 1890. Feature probably named by settlers.

BURRO HILL Between Buffalo Fork and Black Rock Creek. Pop-eye (sometimes called Burro) Smith lived in a dugout cabin, mined for gold and raised burros on his ranch on the Buffalo Fork.

BUTLER CREEK Drains into the Snake River from the southwest near the southern end of Jackson Hole. Named for settler Bill Butler who lived there in 1894.

CACHE CREEK Drains Cache Creek Canyon, which lies at the east end of the town of Jackson. Beaver Dick Leigh told local prospector "Uncle Jack" Davis that horse thieves "cached" their stolen goods on a ranch located on the creek. Named by early settlers.

CAMP CREEK Runs into the Hoback River from the north near Camp Davis *(see Camp Davis)*.

CAMP CREEK SADDLE The divide between the Hoback River and Little Horse Creek. Named after Camp Creek. In this area, two fur trappers, George More and a man from Mississippi named Foy, were killed by Gros Ventre Indians while returning from the Pierre's Hole Rendezvous of 1832.

CAMP DAVIS Located on the south side of the Hoback River. University of Michigan summer science camp. Named after Professor J.B Davis, the former head of the Civil Engineering Department of the University of Michigan.

CARMICHAEL FORK South of Mount Leidy. Named for early settler, C. Carmichael who lived in the valley during the early 1900s. His nephew, Bob Carmichael, operated a fishing guide service on the present sight of the Moose Village Store until his death in 1950. Bob's wife, Fran, was postmaster of Moose.

CARPENTER DRAW On the southwest side of Shadow Mountain near the Park boundary. Named for George E. Carpenter, Teton County Assessor for twenty years, who homesteaded in the valley in 1910.

CARROT KNOLL Lies at the north end of the Teton Range, near the western boundary of the Park, above Conant Pass. Settler's sheep probably denuded the forage until miles of wild carrots, which the sheep would not eat, remained.

CASCADE CANYON The large, glacial carved, U-shaped canyon near the middle of the Teton Range. Named for its creek that cascades dramatically down the canyon and into Jenny Lake.

CASCADE CREEK Enters Jenny Lake from the west. Originally named Glacier Creek by Hayden in 1872. Name changed in 1931 because the creek does not show glacial silt.

CATHEDRAL GROUP Not an officially named feature. Mount Teewinot, the Grand Teton, and Mount Owen appear as cathedral-like spires when viewed from the one-way road north of Jenny Lake, inspiring the name.

CHAPEL OF THE TRANSFIGURATION Located near Menor's Ferry on the Snake River just north of Moose Visitor Center. Log structure built in 1925 with money provided by dude ranchers and neighbors on land donated by Maude Noble. Named by its owner, the Episcopal Church, for the Transfiguration of Christ.

CHRISTIAN POND Between Emma Matilda Lake and Jackson Lake Lodge. Named for Charles A. Christian, commonly known as Tex, the caretaker for Amoretta Inn, which later became the original Jackson Lake Lodge at Moran.

CIRQUE LAKE (el. 9,514') West of Mount Moran, located in a rounded enclosure, or cirque, formed by the head of a glacier that pulled rock from the surrounding walls.

CLEFT FALLS Located in Garnet Canyon. A split falls, as the name suggests.

CLOUDVEIL DOME (el. 12,026') Midway between Nez Perce and the South Teton. Named for its domeshaped summit, frequently cloud veiled. USGB Map, 1931.

COAL MINE DRAW   East of Uhl Hill and northeast of Triangle X Ranch. Coal from the mine was used to power machinery during the construction of Jackson Lake Dam.

COBURN CREEK   Southwest of Munger Mountain, originally called Fall Creek, but the USGB renamed it for Rufus Coburn, first rancher on the creek.

COLES CANYON   Located north of Hoback Junction. Named for a rancher who lived in the canyon for a short while just before World War I.

COLTER BAY   Adjoining Colter Bay Village in the north end of the Park. Created by the rise in Jackson Lake's water level because of Jackson Lake Dam, built in 1916. Named for John Colter, the fur trapper who traveled through the valley during the winter of 1807-1808. Possibly the first white man to visit Jackson Hole. Originally called Mackinaw Bay. Name changed in 1948. Colter Bay Village named for Colter Bay.

COLTER CANYON   Located on the west side of Jackson Lake between Webb and Waterfalls canyons. Named for John Colter *(see Colter Bay).*

COLUMBINE CASCADES   The lower fall of Waterfalls Canyon on the west side of Jackson Lake across the lake from Colter Bay Village. Wild columbine surrounds it in summer.

CONANT BASIN, CREEK, PASS AND TRAIL   On the northwestern edge of the Park. According to Beaver Dick Leigh, named for Al Conant who almost drowned in the creek in 1865. Conant homesteaded on the western side of the Teton Range.

COTTONWOOD CREEK   The cottonwood, Wyoming's state tree, favors streamside growing conditions. There are three Cottonwood Creeks in Jackson Hole: one flows south out of Jenny Lake (called Lake Creek by 1872 Hayden Survey); one flows south into the Gros Ventre River above Upper Slide Lake; and one flows into the Snake River south of Mosquito Creek.

COULTER CREEK   In the Teton Wilderness, eight miles east of the John D. Rockefeller, Jr. Memorial Parkway. Runs into the Snake River just south of the Yellowstone National Park border. Named for John Merle Coulter, botanist of Hayden's 1872 expedition. Shown on GLO maps of 1876.

THE CUNNINGHAM CABIN AS PHOTOGRAPHED BY FRITIOF FRYXELL

PRIOR TO 1940. TWO SUSPECTED HORSE THIEVES,

SPENCER AND BURNETT,

WERE SHOT HERE ON A SPRING MORNING IN 1893.

CRATER LAKE There are two: one is near the old pass road east of Teton Pass. Snowslides formed craters that filled with water from the surrounding cirques. Another is in the Teton Wilderness at the head of the Soda Fork of the Buffalo River.

CUNNINGHAM CABIN HISTORIC SITE Located on the west side of Route 26, just north of Triangle X Ranch. Early homestead of over 500 acres owned by J. Pierce and Margaret Cunningham.

CURTIS CANYON In the Gros Ventre Mountains, adjoining the National Elk Refuge. Named for two brothers, Lysander and Leander Curtis, who bought their ranch from D.C. Nowlin, Wyoming's first game commissioner, at the turn of the century.

CYGNET LAKE A small lake southeast of Colter Bay. Trumpeter swans frequent it and nest there. A cygnet is a young swan.

DALLAS FORK Together with Carmichael Fork forms Slate Creek which drains southward into the Gros Ventre River. Named for professional wolf hunter and trapper Walt Dallas, active during 1914 and 1915.

DARWIN PEAK (el. 11,657′) Located in the Gros Ventre Range, northeast of Granite Creek. Named for an early rancher who settled near the peak. Shown on FS Map of 1912.

DEADHORSE PASS In the Teton Range, just outside the Park, northwest of Mount Moran. Because it was such a dangerous pass for horses, poachers often came into the valley this way, making pursuit by lawmen more difficult.

DEADMAN'S BAR On the Snake River ten miles upstream from Moose Village. Named after John Tonner's three mining companions were found dead there in 1886. There were no witnesses to the crime and although Tonner was arrested, he was freed on the grounds of self-defense.

DEADMAN POINT On Jackson Lake just above Spalding Bay. About 1910, a stranger was snowshoeing down from the head of the lake, got lost in a storm, and froze to death. His body was found at this spot. In the twenties, two men working for ECW (Emergency Conservation Work) got into a fight and one killed the other. Some think the point was named at this time, but it has been called Deadman Point since the 1910 incident.

DEATH CANYON Large Teton canyon that adjoins Phelps Lake.

There are numerous theories about the origin of the name. Perhaps the most plausible contention is that in 1899 a member of Thomas Bannon's survey party wandered into the canyon and was never seen again.

DELTA LAKE On the eastern slope of the Grand Teton at the foot of Teton Glacier. Silt deposited in the lake from the meltwater of the glacier formed a delta at the west end of the lake. USGB Map, 1911.

DISAPPOINTMENT PEAK (el. 11,618′) Named by Phil Smith and Walter Harvey in August, 1925. Thinking the Grand Teton could be climbed by this route, they were disappointed when they found a great gap between them and their summit goal to the northwest.

DITCH CREEK Runs into the Snake River from the east just north of Blacktail Butte. Named for ditches dug by prospectors looking for gold in the 1860s and '70s. GLO map, 1900.

DOANE PEAK (el. 11,354′) Located west of Waterfalls Canyon. Named for army Lieutenant Gustavus C. Doane, a member of the Washburn Langford expedition to Yellowstone in 1870. Formerly called Cairn Peak.

DOLLAR ISLAND A small island northeast of Elk Island on Jackson Lake. Named because of the island's round shape.

DONOHO POINT In the southeastern corner of Jackson Lake. Named for a trapper who lived there around the turn of the century. After the Jackson Lake Dam was built in 1916, the point became an island because of the higher water level.

DUDLEY LAKE (el. 8,243′) On the southern side of Snowshoe Canyon, one mile north of Bivouac Peak. Named in 1970 for Dudley Hayden, second ranger in the new Grand Teton National Park, who discovered the lake in 1912. He served many years as a ranger and fire dispatcher in Grand Teton, and water commissioner for Teton County.

EAGLE'S REST (el. 11,258′) A peak between Waterfalls and Snowshoe canyons. Name probably related to the sighting of a bald eagle perched on a tree on this mountain.

EAST HORN (OF MOUNT MORAN) (el. 10,700′) On the southeast slope of Mount Moran, a rock pinnacle or "horn," on the eastern side of Falling Ice Glacier. West Horn guards

DUDLEY LAKE WAS NAMED IN 1970 TO HONOR DUDLEY HAYDEN

SHOWN HERE GAUGING THE SIZE OF A MATURE

WHITEBARK PINE TREE NEAR THE FORKS OF CASCADE CANYON.

HAYDEN, AN EARLY PARK RANGER,

DISCOVERED THIS HIGH ALPINE LAKE IN 1932.

CRANDALL STUDIO.

the other side of the glacier.

EAST PRONG (el. 11,900') A projecting rocky spur on the ridge between Mount Owen and Mount Teewinot.

ELBOW, THE South of Hoback Junction the Snake River turns west into the canyon at a 90 degree angle to slice through the heart of a great overthrust mountain belt that includes the Snake River Range, the Wyoming Range and Salt River Range.

ELK ISLAND After observing elk swimming to this island, work crews on the Jackson Lake Dam subsequently referred to it as Elk Island.

EMMA MATILDA LAKE North of the Oxbow Bend of the Snake River. Named by W.O. Owen, for his wife. Owen was a topographer for the General Land Office. Owen and his wife attempted an unsuccessful climb on the Grand Teton in 1891. Seven years later Owen was successful.

ENOS LAKE, CREEK In the Teton Wilderness, east of the headwaters of Pacific Creek. Named for John Enos, Shoshoni guide for explorers Bonneville and Fremont in the early 1800s. Enos camped near the lake each summer.

EYNON DRAW North of Spread Creek, southeast of Uhl Hill. Named for John Eynon, an early Jackson Hole rancher. In 1923 Eynon was active in a group of local residents who proposed a plan to limit exploitation of Jackson Hole.

FALL CREEK Runs into the Snake River from the west, just below Hoback Junction. Formerly called Coburn Creek, renamed Fall Creek before 1890 because of its small waterfalls *(see Coburn Creek).*

FALLING ICE GLACIER On the southeastern slope of Mount Moran. The steepest glacier in the range. Frontal ice breaks off and falls. USGB Map, 1931.

FARNEY LAKES Two small lakes north of the upper Gros Ventre River. West of Crystal Creek. Named for Farney Cole, an early valley resident.

FLAT CREEK Runs southeast through the flat meadows of the National Elk Refuge and through the town of Jackson. Orestes St. John of Hayden's 1877 expedition called it Little Gros Ventre Creek. Called Flat Creek of Little Gros Ventre on

GLO plots of 1894. On Forest Service map of 1912, called simply Flat Creek.

FONDA POINT At the mouth of Lizard Creek on the east side of Jackson Lake. Formerly named Lizard Point, it was renamed for Park ranger, John Fonda, who died from exposure after falling through the ice while crossing the lake on a winter ski patrol May 9, 1960 *(see Wilcox Point).*

FORGET-ME-NOT-LAKES In the Teton Range west of Prospectors Mountain. A cluster of small alpine lakes visible from the trail along the Death Canyon Shelf. The lakes take their name from tiny, blue-flowered alpine forget-me-nots that grow at this elevation.

FOSSIL MOUNTAIN (el. 10,800′) Just outside the Park boundary, southwest of Death Canyon. Named for its sedimentary rocks rich in fossils, correcting the impression that there are no fossils in the Teton Range. Mountain contains formations from ancient shallow seas. USGB, 1911.

GARNET CANYON Drains into Bradley Lake. Imperfect garnets up to two and one-half inches in diameter occur at the head of the canyon. Formerly Bradley Canyon. USGB, 1931.

GEORGE'S CANYON Runs off Munger Mountain into the Snake River from the west. Named for George Robinson, a local rancher.

GLACIER FALLS Formed by Glacier Creek which flows from Teton Glacier down Glacier Gulch. Milky water indicated that glacial action above is pulverizing rock into a flour.

GLACIER GULCH Broad, glacier-carved gulch on the east flank of the range, below Teton Glacier.

GLORY, MOUNT North of Teton Pass. Named by members of the University of Michigan at Camp Davis *(see Camp Davis),* who noted its "glorious" appearance. Avalanches from adjacent Glory Bowl often close the road over Teton Pass.

GOODWIN LAKE North of the top of 10,707′ Jackson Peak, which was previously called Goodwin Peak after an old fellow who hunted, guided and camped there around 1904.

GRAND TETON, THE (el. 13,770′) Highest mountain in the Teton Range. Named by French-Canadian trappers of the Hudson Bay Company. Upon viewing the mountains from the broad valley on the west side of the range, these trappers dubbed the South, Middle, and Grand, Les Trois Tetons, or "The Three Breasts." French-Canadian trappers may have spoken of Les Trois Tetons prior to 1800. Indians called the peaks "The Hoary Headed Fathers," also Teewinot (a Shoshoni word meaning many pinnacles). Wilson Price Hunt and the Astorians dubbed the range "The Pilot Knobs" in 1812. Members of F.V. Hayden's 1872 survey named the Grand Teton "Mount Hayden," an honor Hayden himself rejected.

GRANITE BASIN, LAKES West of the western boundary of Grand Teton National Park, northwest of Little's Peak. The rocks are chiefly gneiss, a metamorphic rock, not granite. Called Granite Basin because rocks were misidentified.

GRANITE CANYON, CREEK Runs into the Hoback River from the north above Battle Mountain. Called Cross Creek by Robert Stuart of the American Fur Company in 1812. Named for granite exposures near the headwaters of the creek. Shown on the USGS Map of 1908.

GRANITE CANYON In the southern part of Grand Teton National Park, two miles southwest of Phelps Lake. Comprised chiefly of metamorphic rocks called gneiss. Called Granite Canyon because rocks were misidentified.

GRAVEL MOUNTAIN (el. 9,536′) West of Two Ocean Lake in the Teton Wilderness. Prominent mountain that stands out notably in the summer evening sun. It is composed of durable quartzite pebbles and cobbles that have been washed back and forth across this region throughout the last fifty million years. These rocks have made up various mountains only to be eroded and redistributed time and again. The same type of material covers the floor of Jackson Hole.

GRIZZLY BEAR LAKE West of Mount Woodring. Grizzlies were hunted and occasionally taken in this vicinity of the northern part of the Teton Range prior to the establishment of Grand Teton National Park.

GROS VENTRE BUTTES Northwest of the town of Jackson. East and West Gros Ventre buttes were shown on Hayden's 1877 map as Upper and Lower Gros Ventre buttes. What is now Blacktail Butte was called the North Gros Ventre butte

The Morning After in May, 1925.

The Gros Ventre Landslide dammed the River

and backed up water, submerging most

of the cabin in the right foreground.

BRIDGER-TETON NATIONAL FOREST.

in Bradley's Report, 1872 *(see Gros Ventre Range)*.

GROS VENTRE RANGE, RIVER   (Prefix to many place names). Means "big belly" in French. Two references relate to the origin of the use of this term in the Jackson Hole area. Some historians believe that sign language used by local Indians in the area was misinterpreted by the French to mean "big belly." Others think that the name referred to the swollen stomachs of local Indians that had too little to eat.

GROS VENTRE SLIDE   In 1925 the northern end of Sheep Mountain slid into Gros Ventre Canyon, damming the river to form Lower Slide Lake. The slide is more than a mile long and one-half mile wide. It took only about one and one-half to three minutes for over 20,000 cubic yards of rock to slide into the canyon.

HACKAMORE CREEK   Tributary to the South Fork of the Gros Ventre River. "Hackamore" is of Spanish origin meaning halter, usually of plaited horsehair, with a loop that may be tightened about the nose. Shown on Owen's 1892 Survey and the Mount Leidy Quad. of 1899.

HALF MOON LAKE   East of Moran Junction, south of the Buffalo Fork. An oxbow of the river. A description of its shape. The lake is actually an oxbow created when a bend or meander of a river channel is cut off from the main stream by the deposit of sediment when the river changes its course to a more direct path. Shown on the Mount Leidy Quad., 1899.

HANGING CANYON   Canyon that appears to hang on the southeastern side of Mount St. John. The mouth of this glacier-formed canyon is 1,500 feet above the floor of Jackson Hole.

HANSEN PEAK (el. 7,339')   On West Gros Ventre Butte. Named for Peter C. Hansen, an early settler who came to live in Jackson Hole in 1907. He helped build the first Jackson Lake Dam and was one of the early mail carriers in the valley. Former Wyoming Senator Clifford Hansen is his son.

HAREM HILL (el. 7,330')   On the northwestern side of Jackson Lake below the inlet. Presumably, the name derives from elk, not humans. During the rut (fall mating season), bull elk gather harems of ten to twenty cows. Each dominant bull will "defend" his harem by bugling and displaying his antlers. Actual combat between bull elk over possession of a harem is rare.

HECHTMAN CREEK, LAKE   North of Berry Creek. Named for a trapper who got caught in a snowslide in the early part of 1900. Hechtman Creek runs into Berry Creek.

HEDRICK POND, SPRING   Small lake, point and spring southwest of Triangle X Ranch named for early resident Charles Hedrick. Before coming to Jackson Hole, Hedrick was clawed by a grizzly. He grew a beard to hide his scars. He entered Jackson Hole over Togwotee Pass in 1896. There was no road, just an old Indian and trapper trail. He homesteaded near the spring but later sold his homestead. The lake was previously called Pingress Lake. Shown on the Presidential proclamation map of 1904.

HERMITAGE POINT   Large point of land on the eastern side of Jackson Lake between Donoho Point and Elk Island. A now unknown builder intended to use the site for a lodge or hermitage. After the dam was built in 1916, he floated the logs down river and sold them.

HIDDEN FALLS   On Cascade Creek, just west of Jenny Lake. A favorite recreation spot of the settlers. Named by early settlers, the falls could not be seen from the road on the eastern side of Jenny Lake.

HOLLY LAKE   Small lake lying in a glacial cirque near the head of Indian Paintbrush Canyon. Named for Holly Leek, a lifelong Jackson Hole resident and son of Stephen Leek. The lake was named by Glen Crosby, friend and coworker of Holly.

HOBACK CANYON   Southeast of Jackson Hole. Canyon takes its name from the river *(see Hoback River)*.

HOBACK RIVER   Runs into the Snake River from the east before the Snake River turns west at the Elbow. Named by Wilson Price Hunt of the Overland Astorian party for his guide John Hoback. In 1811 Hoback and his two companions, John Robinson and John Reznor, enlisted with Hunt's party and guided them across northern Wyoming, over Union Pass, down the Hoback River, and over Teton Pass to Andrew Henry's fort in Idaho.

HOLMES CAVE   At the head of Holmes Cave Creek, north of Togwotee Pass. Discovered by Edwin Holmes of Brookline,

CHARLEY HEDRICK, AN EARLY HOMESTEADER WHO FIRST

CAME TO JACKSON HOLE IN 1896, BUILT HIS CABIN NEAR THE

POND AND SPRING WHICH BEAR HIS NAME.

TETON COUNTY LIBRARY BICENTENNIAL PHOTO COLLECTION AND
THE TETON COUNTY HISTORICAL SOCIETY.

Massachusetts, in 1898 when he came to Jackson Hole to hunt. First Jackson Hole settler, John Holland, was his guide. Holmes returned to Jackson Hole in 1905, and he and Holland finished exploring the cave.

HORSE CREEK   Runs into the Snake River from the east, just above Hoback Junction. It was an alternate Indian and trapper horse trail to the Green River.

HORSETHIEF CANYON   At the south end of Jackson Hole. Runs into the Snake River from the east. John Wilson of Jackson Hole found a cache of branding irons at this site. All brands were strange to Jackson Hole. Horsethieves probably used the canyon as a hide-out.

HOUSETOP MOUNTAIN (el. 10,537′)   On the hydrographic divide of the Teton Range, outside the Park just west of Marion Lake. Named for its houselike appearance. USGS map, 1908.

HUCKLEBERRY HOT SPRINGS   West of Flagg Ranch in the John D. Rockefeller, Jr. Memorial Parkway. Unlike other hot springs *(see Granite and Astoria)*, these springs are heated by now-buried and still-cooling lava flows. Named Huckleberry, probably for Huckleberry Mountain, in the 1960s when the resort area was developed under lease from the U.S. Forest Service. In 1935, Allen and Day, thermal investigators in Yellowstone, had previously named them Polecat Spings. Before that they had been known as Flagg Ranch Hot Springs.

HUCKLEBERRY MOUNTAIN (el. 9,409′)   Northeast of Steamboat Mountain, where huckleberries grow in profusion. The tusk hunters in the early part of the century built hideaways there. Called Soldier Hill in the twenties *(see Purdy Creek and Basin)*. First shown on Yellowstone Park Timber and Land map of 1899.

HUNT, MOUNT (el. 10,783′)   Between Open and Granite canyons in the Teton Range. Named in recognition of Wilson Price Hunt, who led the Astorians through Jackson Hole in 1811. USGB, 1931.

HURRICANE PASS (el. 10,600′)   West of the Middle Teton on the western edge of the Park. At this high elevation, the exposed pass is subject to high winds, rain, and snowstorms throughout the year.

IWW CREEK   Flows into Lower Slide Lake in the Gros Ventre Mountains from the north. Forest Service employees building a trail along the creek decided the work was not to their liking. Recalling the International Workers of the World slogan, "I Won't Work," they named the nearby creek IWW according to oldtimer Joe May.

ICEFLOE LAKE (el. 10,649′)   West of the Middle Teton. In the summer the lake thaws out but nearly always contains ice floes, flat masses of floating ice.

ICE POINT   Sharp pinnacle between Storm Point and Symmetry Spire. Named following the first ascent on August 13, 1931, by ranger naturalist Fritiof Fryxell and ranger Frank Smith when the pinnacle was sheathed in ice.

INDIAN ISLAND   Small island in Jackson Lake near the mouth of Arizona Creek. Before Jackson Lake Dam was built, the island was part of the shoreline. It was a popular summer Indian campsite, located along a traditional route running from Pacific Creek to Berry Creek and across the northern end of the Teton Range into present-day Idaho.

INDIAN PAINTBRUSH CANYON   Drains northeast into Leigh Lake. Indian paintbrush, the state flower of Wyoming, colors the lower portions of the canyon during the summer. Name approved in 1931.

INSPIRATION POINT   On the western shore of Jenny Lake. Offers a beautiful, panoramic view of Jackson Hole.

JACKSON   Largest town and county seat of Teton County, Wyoming. Named for David E. Jackson, who trapped in the area in the mid-1800s. The town was laid out in 1901 by Robert E. Miller.

JACKSON HOLE   Valley on east side of the Teton Range. Fur trappers called a mountain-ringed valley a "hole." Named Jackson's Hole for trapper David E. Jackson. Lately, shortened to Jackson Hole.

JACKSON LAKE   Largest lake in Jackson Hole, on the west side of the valley. At the time of Hayden's explorations in the 1870s, the natural lake surface was about half the size of today's reservoir. Through the years it has been given various names. First, the man who edited the Lewis and Clark journals called

THE TOWN SQUARE OF JACKSON AS

PHOTOGRAPHED IN THE EARLY 1920s.

MRS. VILATE SEATON MORRIS ALBUM.

it Lake Biddle. Next, W.A. Ferris of the American Fur Company called it Teton Lake. In 1829 William Sublette bestowed the final accolade, Jackson Lake, after David E. Jackson, one of his partners in the Rocky Mountain Fur Company *(see Jackson Lake Dam)*.

JACKSON LAKE DAM   Built on the Snake River west of Moran Junction. The first reservoir was formed by a log crib built by the U.S. Reclamation Service in 1906, with a storage capacity of 300,000 acre feet. The dam washed out in 1910 and was replaced by an earthen dam built by Frank T. Crow in 1916, which raised the natural lake level 39 feet and increased the capacity of the lake to 790,000 acre feet. In 1917, by dredging the outlet, it was further increased to 847,000 acre feet. Water is stored for irrigation in Idaho.

JACKSON PEAK (el. 10,741′)   East of the town of Jackson. First called Goodwin Peak for an old timer who camped, guided and lived there early in the century. The peak was later named after Teton Jackson, an outlaw, rather than for David Jackson.

JEDEDIAH SMITH, MOUNT (el. 10,610′)   Directly west of Mount Meek. Named for famed fur trapper, Jedediah Strong Smith, active in the west in the 1820s and 30s, as a partner with David Jackson and William Sublette in the Rocky Mountain Fur Company. Smith was the first to cross South Pass from the east and recognize its significance as a route. He was also the first to travel overland to California. In 1831 he was killed by Comanches on the Santa Fe Trail.

JEDEDIAH SMITH WILDERNESS   Wilderness area in the Targhee National Forest. Named in honor of Jedediah Smith *(see Mount Jedediah Smith)*.

JENNY LAKE   Piedmont lake at the mouth of Mount Teewinot. Named by Hayden in 1872 for Jenny, the Shoshoni wife of his guide, Beaver Dick Leigh. She pitched the tents, cooked the food, and kept her family in hand. All members of the Hayden party had nothing but praise for her. In 1876 Jenny and her six children died of smallpox.

JOHN D. ROCKEFELLER, JR. MEMORIAL PARKWAY   This National Recreation Area, between Grand Teton National Park and Yellowstone National Park, was set aside in 1972 and

This photo, taken in 1933, shows visitors enjoying the view of Jenny Lake and Cascade Canyon. Although the dress and the appearance of Park Visitors have changed since this time, the ageless beauty of the mountains and the quiet awe that they inspire in all remain unaltered.

CRANDALL STUDIO

named to honor John D. Rockefeller, Jr. A well known philanthropist, Rockefeller was also a conservationist whose gifts of land made possible the creation or expansion of Acadia, Great Smokey Mountain, Grand Teton, and Virgin Islands national parks.

JOY CREEK, LAKES, AND PEAK   Joy Creek runs into the North Buffalo Fork. Joy Peak (el. 10,041′) is southeast of the Buffalo Fork. All named for Louis H. Joy, one of the first dude ranchers in Jackson Hole. In 1908 he established the JY Ranch which is now owned by the Rockefellers.

KELLY   Small Jackson Hole community fifteen miles northeast of Jackson. Founded by William Kelly when he built a sawmill there in 1907. A post office was built in 1914 with B.F. Goe as postmaster. Kelly was nearly voted the county seat of Teton County in 1925. Only two buildings, the school and Trinity Episcopal Church, were left standing after the Gros Ventre flood in 1927.

KINKY CREEK   South of Bacon Ridge. Runs into the upper Gros Ventre River. An old Indian and trapper trail into Jackson Hole runs along the tightly meandering creek.

KIT LAKE   Small lake in the Teton Range, north of Snowdrift Lake. Young beaver and otter are called kits.

LAKE CREEK   There are two: an affluent of the Gros Ventre River, flows into Upper Slide Lake; another, drains Phelps Lake.

LAKE OF THE CRAGS   Highest of three lakes in Hanging Canyon. Lies far above timberline and is surrounded on all sides but the east by bristling crags. USGB, 1931.

LAFFERTY CREEK   Drains into the upper Gros Ventre River. Named for W.D. Lafferty, a turn-of-the-century pioneer.

LAUREL LAKE   About three-fourths of a mile above and west of String Lake. The mountain slopes are densely grown with ceanothus, commonly called laurel. USGB, 1931.

LEEKS CANYON   First canyon on the east side of Highway 26 south of Jackson. S.N. Leek settled in the valley before the turn of the century. His photographs of starving elk and his lectures in the East on their plight were largely responsible for the establishment of the National Elk Refuge. Leek's ranch was near the canyon.

"Two Old Timers."

Stephen N. Leek came to Jackson Hole

to settle prior to 1900. He was instrumental in the

establishment of The National Elk Refuge.

LEIDY, MOUNT (el. 10,326′) Prominent peak east of Antelope Flats. Named by Hayden in 1872 for professor Joseph Leidy, comparative anatomist and paleontologist. Leidy was also in Hayden's 1878 party and was with Raynolds in Jackson Hole in 1860. Mount Moran was once called Mount Leidy by Bradley, the chief geologist with the Hayden survey in 1872.

LEIGH CANYON, CREEK Creek runs from west to east into Leigh Lake south of Mount Moran. Named for Beaver Dick Leigh, guide of Hayden's 1872 expedition. In 1876 Dick's Shoshoni wife, whom he called Jenny, and their six children died of smallpox. A few years later, Beaver Dick married a Bannock named Sioux Tadpole, by whom he had three children: Emma, Bill and Rosa. First shown on the USGS Map, 1901.

LEIGH LAKE South of Jackson Lake. Named for Hayden's guide, Beaver Dick Leigh (see Leigh Canyon).

LILY LAKE On Spread Creek, south of Baldy Mountain. Named for its yellow pond lilies that thrive during the summer. Mount Leidy Quad for 1899.

LITTLE MACKINAW BAY On the eastern side of Jackson Lake below Colter Bay. Named for the Mackinaw trout. This exotic fish was planted in Shoshone Lake in southern Yellowstone Park in the late 1800s by the Army, which was then administering the Park. By the 1890s the trout had migrated from Shoshone Lake down the Snake River into Jackson Lake and up Cottonwood Creek into Leigh, String and Jenny lakes. Today, national park policies do not permit the stocking of a non-native species of fish or the stocking of lakes that are naturally barren of fish.

LITTLE'S PEAK (el. 10,712′) On the western edge of Grand Teton National Park. Probably named for E.N. Little, a mountaineer who climbed in the Tetons in 1911. Presumably the first ascent was made by T.M. Bannon's party of 1898, as their topographic map shows a bench mark on the summit. Forest Service map of 1920.

LIZARD CREEK Runs into the eastern side of Jackson Lake below Fonda Point. Salamanders were probably mistaken for lizards. Yellowstone Timber and Land map of 1899.

LLOYD CREEK Runs into the upper Gros Ventre River from

BEAVER DICK LEIGH, HIS INDIAN WIFE JENNY AND CHILDREN

PHOTOGRAPHED ON THE SHOSHONI INDIAN RESERVATION BY

WILLIAM H. JACKSON IN 1876. LEIGH SERVED AS GUIDE TO FRANK

BRADLEY AND MEMBERS OF THE HAYDEN EXPEDITION IN 1872 WHILE

THEY WERE IN JACKSON HOLE. THE SURVEY NAMED LEIGH AND JENNY

LAKES TO HONOR THIS TRAPPER AND HIS SQUAW.

the southeast. Named for Theophilous W. Lloyd (most of the settlers called him "T.W.") who had a ranch there from 1910-1920. He started a guide club in Jackson in 1912.

LOOKOUT (el. 8,383′) On Munger Mountain. Used as a Forest Service fire lookout location.

LOST CREEK Runs from the highlands north of Shadow Mountain. Disappears underground on its way to the Snake River.

LOWER SLIDE LAKE East of Kelly. In 1925 the Gros Ventre Slide dammed the Gros Ventre River to form the lake *(see Gros Ventre Slide)*.

LOZIER HILL (el. 7,655′) Located south of Emma Matilda Lake. Named for an early settler, Roy Lozier, of Moran, who had a homestead south of Emma Matilda Lake around 1910.

LUNCH TREE HILL Overlooks Jackson Lake Lodge. This was a favorite luncheon spot for J.D. Rockefeller, Jr. *(see John D. Rockefeller, Jr. Memorial Parkway)*.

LUPINE MEADOWS East of Teewinot Mountain and south of Jenny Lake. Lavender blue lupine bloom here in profusion in early summer.

MACLEOD LAKE East of Granite Hot Springs. Named for Dr. D.G. MacLeod, one of the valley's first resident doctors, who came to Jackson Hole in the 1930s.

MARION LAKE At the upper end of Granite Canyon. Named for Marion Danford, of Philadelphia, who came as a dude to the Bar BC Ranch around 1915. She later became the owner of the D Triangle Ranch.

MEADOWS, THE On upper Crystal Creek in the Gros Ventre Range. An open area used by early outfitters' as a campground and as a summer campsite by Sheepeater Indians.

MEEK, MOUNT (el. 10,677′) On the southwestern boundary of Grand Teton National Park. Memorializes fur trapper Joe Meek, who first visited Jackson Hole in 1829.

MENOR'S FERRY William Menor came to Jackson Hole in 1894 and built a ferry at Moose, one of the few places the Snake River kept to a single channel. The ferry provided a convenient and safe crossing. Menor sold the ferry and homestead to Maude Noble in 1918. She operated the ferry

BILL MENOR'S HOMESTEAD, SEEN HERE FROM THE EAST BANK OF THE

SNAKE RIVER, AS IT APPEARED IN 1898. MENOR WAS MOOSE JUNCTION'S

FIRST SETTLER. TODAY HIS HOME IS AN HISTORIC SITE

PRESERVED NEAR GRAND TETON NATIONAL PARK HEADQUARTERS.

STIMSON COLLECTION, WYOMING STATE ARCHIVES AND HISTORICAL DEPARTMENT.

until 1927, when a steel-truss bridge rendered it obsolete.

MICA LAKE (el. 9,543′) On a high bench south of Lake Solitude. Mica is a common mineral of the crystalline rocks of the Teton Range. Large flaky crystals are seen in the pegmatite dikes and glistening on sections of the trail. These nearly transparent sheets of muscovite, called isinglass, were used early in the century in the doors of potbelly stoves, in carriage windows and as electrical insulation. The name is probably drived from the Latin *micare*, meaning to flash or sparkle.

MIDDLE TETON (el. 12,700′) The middle summit of the historic Trois Tetons. Recognizable by the vertical black diabase dike on its eastern face.

MILL CREEK Tributary of Mosquito Creek in southwestern Jackson Hole. Named because of the early sawmill built by a man named Johnson.

MILLER BUTTE, SPRINGS On the National Elk Refuge north of Jackson. Named for Robert E. Miller, first president of Jackson State Bank, first supervisor of Teton National Forest, and one of the valley's earliest prominent men. He homesteaded in 1885 and remained in Jackson Hole until he died in 1934 at the age of 71.

MILLER CABIN HISTORICAL SITE Located on the National Elk Refuge east of Jackson. The homestead of Robert Miller *(see Miller Butte).*

MINER CREEK (WEST AND EAST) Runs into the Gros Ventre River from the south, above Slide Lake. Named for Bill Miner, a local carpenter.

MINK LAKE (el. 8,890′) At the head of Leigh Canyon. Name probably relates to the sighting of mink, a member of the weasel family seldom seen in the Park. Shown on the GLO plot for 1900.

MOOSE VILLAGE Small community located twelve miles north of Jackson. Includes visitor center, park headquarters, store, post office and gas station. Moose frequent the area, particularly during the winter and spring. Originally called Menor's Ferry, the name was changed to Moose at the request of the U.S. Postal Service *(see Menor's Ferry).*

MORAN Small town formerly located just east of Jackson Lake

BILL MENOR AT THE HELM OF HIS SNAKE RIVER FERRY.

BILL SETTLED IN JACKSON HOLE IN 1892 AND ESTABLISHED

MENOR'S FERRY CROSSING WHICH WOULD SERVE JACKSON HOLE

SETTLERS UNTIL 1927 WHEN A BRIDGE WAS COMPLETED

AT MOOSE JUNCTION.

Dam. Named for Mount Moran. The first building there was Cap Smith's Hotel, a two-story log structure constructed in 1902. The town was named by Maria Allen, who served as the postmaster until 1906 when the job went to Ben Sheffield. Charlie Fesler took over the management of the store in 1924 and the post office in 1929. The town was dismantled in 1957. Today Moran is a post office, school, and small park employee housing area near Moran Junction *(see Mount Moran)*.

MORAN BAY   A bay indenting the western shore of Jackson Lake at the base of Mount Moran. Named for Mount Moran. Lt. Doane called it Spirit Bay because of the echoes in the bay, and it has also been called Swimming Moose Bay.

MORAN CANYON   The U-shaped canyon between Mount Moran and Bivouac Peak. Named for Mount Moran by T.M. Bannon of the USGS in 1898-99.

MORAN CREEK   Flows down Moran Canyon into Jackson Lake. Named for Mount Moran and approved by USGB Map, 1931.

MORAN, MOUNT (el. 12,605′)   Most prominent peak in the northern end of the Teton Range. Named by Ferdinand V. Hayden for the landscape artist Thomas Moran. Frank Bradley called the mountain Mount Leidy in his 1872 report. Shown as Mount Moran on Orestes St. John's 1877 map. Moran traveled with the 1872 Hayden expedition into Yellowstone and into Pierre's Hole on the western side of the Teton Range. He produced many sketches and watercolors from these travels.

MORMON ROW   Rich former farming district east of Blacktail Butte settled by Mormons. The soil in some places is many feet deep.

MUNGER MOUNTAIN (el. 8,316′)   Between Fall Creek and the Snake River. Named for William Munger, a placer miner who came to the area in the early 1890s.

NATIONAL ELK REFUGE   Northeast of Jackson. Administered by the U.S. Fish and Wildlife Service, Congress created the Refuge in 1912. In 1900 as the elk herds migrated south after summering in Yellowstone National Park, fences and other developments blocked their traditional routes. Around 1910 elk wintering in Jackson Hole were competing with cattle for

ARTIST THOMAS MORAN, PICTURED IN FRONT OF HIS TENT,

WAS A MEMBER OF THE 1872 HAYDEN EXPEDITION.

DURING HIS TRAVELS WITH THE SURVEY GROUP,

MORAN PAINTED IMPRESSIVE WATERCOLORS

OF YELLOWSTONE AND OF THE TETON PEAKS.

MT. MORAN HONORS HIS NAME.

forage and feeding on ranchers' haystacks. Hundreds of elk died of starvation each winter. Local residents became very concerned. Stephen N. Leek photographed starving and dead elk and traveled east to publicize the tragedy. As a result of his work the National Elk Refuge was created. The refuge has expanded from a modest 2,760 acres to over 24,000 acres today.

NEZ PERCE (el. 11,700') Southeast of the Grand Teton. Named for an Indian tribe whose well known leader was Chief Joseph. Sometimes referred to as Howling Dog Mountain because of the resemblance when seen from the north.

NOKER MINE DRAW On Cache Creek. Named for John Noker, a coal miner on Little Granite and Cache creeks in the 1940s. When oil became the popular heating fuel, he closed his mines.

OPEN CANYON This wide, glaciated canyon is located south of Death Canyon and Phelps Lake. First shown on the USGS Map of 1901 according to Dr. Fritiof Fryxell, the name was approved in 1911.

OPEN DOOR Mountain above Granite Hot Springs. When approached from the south, a vertical slab or chimney of rock resembles an open door.

OUZEL FALLS On the upper Gros Ventre River. Named for the water ouzel or dipper. This bird lives and nests along fast running streams and even feeds underwater on insects.

OWEN, MOUNT (el. 12,928') Neighboring peak of the Grand Teton to the northeast. Named for W.O. Owen, who climbed the Grand Teton in 1898 with Bishop Spalding, John Shive, and Frank Petersen. Approved by USGB 1927.

OXBOW BEND An oxbow of the Snake River directly east of Jackson Lake Dam. Its shape resembles a pioneer's oxbow. Geologically speaking, an oxbow is created when a bend or meander of a river channel is cut off from the main stream by the deposit of sediment when the river changes its course to a more direct path. Herons, ospreys, bald eagles, trumpeter swans, geese, ducks, otter and moose frequent the area.

PACIFIC CREEK Tributary of the Snake River, whose waters eventually flow into the Pacific Ocean. Begins at Two Ocean Pass on the Continental Divide. Its counterpart is Atlantic Creek whose waters flow into the Atlantic. Shown on Raynolds' 1859

THIS PHOTO WAS TAKEN AUGUST 11, 1898, DURING THE

FIRST RECOGNIZED ASCENT OF THE GRAND TETON.

W.O. OWEN'S CLIMBING COMPANIONS, BISHOP FRANKLIN SPALDING,

JOHN SHIVE, AND FRANK PETERSEN, ARE SHOWN

ON THE SUMMIT OF THE GRAND.

PHOTO BY WILLIAM OWEN.

map of the Yellowstone and Missouri rivers.

PAINTBRUSH DIVIDE (el. 10,720') Separates Indian Paintbrush Canyon and Cascade Canyon. Named for Indian Paintbrush Canyon *(see Indian Paintbrush Canyon)*.

PASS LAKE South of Fossil Mountain on the mountain pass between Death Canyon and Fox Creek. First shown on the USGS map of 1908.

PELICAN BAY On the eastern side of Jackson Lake just north of Colter Bay. White pelicans can be observed on or near Jackson Lake during the spring and fall.

PENDERGRAFT PEAK Small peak northeast of Togwotee Pass. Named for "Slim" Pendergraft, a Jackson Hole game warden from 1920-50. Pendergraft Meadows are below the peak.

PETERSEN GLACIER Glacier on the western side of the northern fork of Cascade Canyon. Named in honor of Frank Petersen, early homesteader and member of the Owen's party that made the 1898 ascent of the Grand Teton.

PHELPS LAKE (el. 6,633') At the mouth of Death Canyon. Named by F.V. Hayden. According to Beaver Dick Leigh, Phelps trapped in the area for years. His full name is not known. USGB 1931 *(see Phillips Pass)*.

PHILLIPS CANYON, RIDGE Runs from the southwest toward Fish Creek, north of Wilson, Wyoming. Named for a trapper from Teton Basin, the old Pierre's Hole, who built a shack at the mouth of the canyon about 1896. He fished and hunted there for one season *(see Phillips Pass)*.

PHILLIPS PASS (el. 8,932') Historians believe the pass, ridge and Phelps Lake were named after the same man. Beaver Dick Leigh was an original speller, and in his diary (which he spelled "dyra") the name was spelled "Phelps" *(see Phelps Lake)*.

PILGRIM CREEK In northern Jackson Hole. Those who traveled through Jackson Hole by wagon to reach Yellowstone were called "pilgrims" by the settlers. Nearby Pilgrim Mountain (el. 8,274') probably named for the same reason.

POISON CREEK There are two Poison creeks: one runs into Bacon Creek on the upper Gros Ventre River; the other enters the Hoback River near Camp Davis. Both refer to the larkspur, a plant poisonous to stock.

POTHOLES, THE Glacial knob and kettle topography southeast of Jackson Lake. Caused by the melting of huge chunks of stagnant ice that were partly buried by outwash gravel from a huge melting glacier. The potholes is a local name referring to the large depressions in this part of the Park's landscape. USBGN named the area "Pitted Plain" in 1931; changed it to "Potholes" in 1961.

PROSPECTORS MOUNTAIN (el. 11,000') Between Death and Open canyons. There are no known mineral resources on this mountain. Prospectors in the 1870s and 1880s found Jackson Hole a disappointing source of wealth. However, this peak was named to commemorate the discovery of minerals in Death Canyon. A galena mine was worked for several years in Death Canyon around the turn of the century.

PURDY CREEK, BASIN Creek drains into the south fork of the Gros Ventre River. Charles Purdy, and Bill Binkley were tusk hunters who killed elk only for their tusks, or eye teeth. Elk tusks were the insignia of the BPOE (Elks Club). Tusk hunting was illegal, but convictions were hard to get as tusks could be obtained legally. Locally, concerned Jackson residents handled the situation this way: Everyone was invited to a meeting called a "citizens committee." Otho Williams was elected chairman and announced, "Anyone not willing to take hold of a rope can leave the meeting." No one left, and three men were chosen to go to the cabin of William Binkley, the foremost tusker, without guns and demand that the tuskers leave the valley. They did. However, tusking was not stopped until Wyoming game warden D.C. Nowlin, who lived in Jackson, persuaded the BPOE to give up the elk tusk as an emblem of their organization.

RAMSHEAD LAKE Middle of three lakes in Hanging Canyon. The skull of a large bighorn ram was found near the edge of the lake by a party of mountain climbers. USGB, 1931.

RAMMEL MOUNTAIN (el. 10,140') In the Teton Range, outside the Park, northwest of Snowshoe Canyon. Forest Service maintains a radio relay station on this mountain. A Charles A. Rammel had a mining claim in Jackson Hole in 1912.

RANDOLPH, MOUNT (el. 9,180') Between Lava and Box

THIS TURN-OF-THE-CENTURY PROSPECTOR'S CABIN BUILT AT THE HEAD OF DEATH CANYON IS TESTIMONY TO THE SHATTERED HOPES OF EARLY PROSPECTORS IN JACKSON HOLE. A GALENA MINE WAS WORKED FOR A FEW YEARS IN THE EARLY 1900s IN DEATH CANYON, BUT THE SEARCH FOR THE SOURCE OF GOLD TRACES IN VALLEY STREAMS PROVED UNPRODUCTIVE. TODAY THE OLD CABIN IS GONE, AND ONLY A FEW LOGS REMAIN. PROSPECTOR MOUNTAIN IS LOCATED NEAR THE MOUTH OF DEATH CANYON.

creeks, north of the Buffalo Fork. Named for a homesteader and poacher who was the bane of forest ranger Rudolph Rosencranz's existence *(see Rosie's Ridge)*.

RANGER PEAK (el. 11,355')   In the northern part of the Teton Range, northwest of Waterfalls Canyon. Named in the 1930s to honor the rangers of Grand Teton National Park circa 1930.

RAYNOLDS PEAK (el. 10,905')   West of Bivouac Peak. Named in honor of Captain W.F. Raynolds who explored this region in 1860.

RED HILLS   On the Gros Ventre River above Lower Slide Lake. Part of the Chugwater Formation, which dates from Triassic times, 200 million years ago. These reddish-rock formations are found over much of Wyoming and the United States. W.A. Ferris described the Red Hills in his journal in 1833.

RED SENTINEL, THE   This pinnacle lies on the ridge connecting Disappointment Peak with the Grand Teton. Hans Kraus, a climber who never made the summit, named the peak for its reddish color in 1941.

RED TOP MEADOWS   West of Munger Mountain. Named for red-topped grass covering the meadow.

RIMROCK LAKE (el. 9,700')   A cirque lake high on the south rim of Death Canyon.

ROCKCHUCK PEAK (el. 11,144')   High above and west of String Lake. Rockchuck is a nickname for the marmots that abound on its slopes.

ROSIE'S RIDGE   Runs east-west, between Blackrock Creek and the Buffalo Fork. Named for Rudolph Rosencranz, Teton National Forest ranger. He built the first ranger station on Blackrock Creek and served there from 1904-1927.

SAINT JOHN, MOUNT (el. 11,430')   Between Cascade and Indian Paintbrush canyons. Actually a series of peaks of nearly equal height. Named for Orestes St. John, geologist of Hayden's 1877 survey, whose monographs on the Teton and Wind River ranges are now classics. USGB, 1931.

SARGENT'S BAY   On the eastern shore of Jackson Lake above Leeks Marina. John D. Sargent and Robert Ray Hamilton built a luxurious ten-room log house in the 1880s. Both men were black sheep of famous families: Sargent, a descendant of John Singer Sargent and Hamilton, a descendant of Alexander Hamilton. Sargent is suspected of murdering his partner Hamilton *(see Signal Mountain)*.

SAWMILL PONDS   One mile southeast of Moose on the east side of the Moose-Wilson Road. Al Young had a sawmill located at Huckleberry Springs. These springs are the source of the beaver impounded ponds. Sawing was discontinued when the Park was established in 1929.

SCHOOLROOM GLACIER   Lies at the head of the South Fork of Cascade Canyon, on the eastern slope of Hurricane Pass. Called schoolroom because it is a textbook example of glacial features, including a bergschrund, crevasses, moraines, pedestal boulders, and a small lake at its base colored milky blue by the rock flour suspended in the meltwater.

SHADOW MOUNTAIN   Also called Antelope Mountain. Flanks Jackson Hole on the east. The shadow of the Teton Range stretches across the floor of Jackson Hole in the late afternoon to the aspen-covered slopes of this mountain.

SHADOW PEAK (SHADOW POINT) (el. 10,725')   Southeast of Nez Perce in the Teton Range. Although the official name was approved by USGB in 1931 as Shadow Point, the name on USGS topographic maps remains as Shadow Peak. The summer afternoon shadow of Nez Perce covers Shadow Peak, reducing visibility.

SHEFFIELD ISLAND   Small island near the eastern shore of Jackson Lake named for Ben Sheffield. Sheffield came to Jackson Hole in 1905. As owner of a motel and cabins at the old townsite of Moran, he established himself as a guide for wealthy hunters and "dudes" from the east.

SHEEP MOUNTAIN (el. 11,219')   Part of the Gros Ventre Range, on the east side of Jackson Hole. Named for the Rocky Mountain bighorn sheep that sometimes can be seen on its slopes. Also unofficially called "The Sleeping Indian" because it resembles an Indian chief attired in a feather headdress, stretched out on his back *(see Gros Ventre Slide)*.

SHERIDAN PASS (el. 9,245')   Mountain pass through Wind River Range, nine miles south of Togwotee Pass. General Phillip Sheridan, vigorous supporter of the preservation of Yellowstone

President Chester A. Arthur's Party as photographed in 1883

during their expedition through Yellowstone and Jackson Hole.

The President is seated in the center. Although the Presidential

Party established six different camps along The Gros Ventre

River and in Jackson Hole, no place names bestowed

by Arthur's Expedition have survived.

National Park, accompanied President Chester A. Arthur on his trip through Jackson Hole and Yellowstone in 1883. Robert Lincoln, son of Abraham Lincoln, was also in Arthur's party, and at that time the pass was named Robert A. Lincoln Pass. Many felt that name should have been retained.

SHORTY CREEK   Drains into Crystal Creek on the southern side of the Gros Ventre River. Morris Williams, who owned a pool hall in Jackson, was known as "Shorty."

SHOSHOKO FALLS   Located near the outlet of Lake Taminah in Avalanche Canyon. Shoshoko is a Shoshoni word meaning "walker" which described Indians who were without horses. Visible from the Bradley Lake trail.

SIGNAL MOUNTAIN (el. 7,731')   Near the southeastern tip of Jackson Lake. In 1891 Robert Ray Hamilton was reported lost in Jackson Hole while hunting. Searchers agreed to light a signal fire on the summit of this mountain when he was found. The mountain's commanding location assured that the fire's smoke could be seen by the search parties spread out on the flats below. Seven days later, Hamilton's drowned body was discovered two miles down river from the Jackson Lake outlet *(see also Sargent's Bay)*.

SLEEPING INDIAN MOUNTAIN   *(See Sheep Mountain.)*

SNAKE RIVER   The Snake River originates in the Teton Wilderness in the Bridger-Teton National Forest. After meandering into Yellowstone National Park, it flows into Jackson Lake, exits at the dam, diagonally bisects Jackson Hole, and crosses Idaho to join the Columbia, which empties into the Pacific.

It is important to establish what the name Snake River does not mean. Snake is neither reference to the braided, twisting channels of the river, nor does it have anything to do with reptiles.

Lewis and Clark first encountered the river in 1805. Clark named it Lewis River to honor his companion. Bonneville and Fremont both continued this name in their maps and journals of exploration. However the name Lewis River did not come into common usage among the fur trappers of the region.

French fur trappers called it La Maudite Riviere Enragee

meaning "The Accursed Mad River," because of the difficulty they had negotiating its white-water rapids and falls. The parties of William Price Hunt and Andrew Henry both referred to the upper Snake as Mad River.

Various Indian names were applied to the Snake River by groups of Bannocks, Shoshonis, and Paiutes who lived along its water. These included Yam-pa-pah, an important food plant that grew along the river banks; Lewis and Clark first called the river Kimooenem in their journal; Po-ho-gwa, meaning sagebrush river; and Sho-sho-ne-pah, a reference to the Snake or Shoshoni Indians. It is from this Indian derivation that the river received its permanent name "Snake."

The many names of this river would not indicate historical confusion or disagreement, but rather a tendency of Indian tribes to call a certain section of a stream by a locally descriptive name, as well as the difficulty early explorers had in identifying streams and rivers with their often inadequate or incorrect maps.

SNOWDRIFT LAKE   Lies at the head of Avalanche Canyon and drains into Lake Taminah. Alpine lake surrounded by snowdrifts throughout the year.

SNOW KING MOUNTAIN (el. 7,940′) Flanks the town of Jackson. Called Snow King because of the great amount of snow it receives. Named by Dr. Floyd Kaegal, a developer of the present ski area. Once known as Kelly's Hill after Bill Kelly, a rancher. Also called Mount Ruth Helen McCormick during the 1920s. McCormick helped to develop it as a ski area.

SNOWSHOE CANYON   North of Moran Canyon, northeast of Bivouac Peak. In early days patrol cabins were called snowshoe cabins, referring to the method of getting to them during the winter. The snowshoe cabin remaining at the edge of Moran Bay, at the mouth of Snowshoe Canyon, probably was the source of the canyon's name.

SODA CREEK, LAKE AND POINT   South of the Gros Ventre River above Upper Slide Lake. Named because of the sodium sulfate that collects in the lake and stream from surrounding rock formations. Soda Point (el. 8,260′), probably named for Soda Lake.

SOLDIER MEADOWS   Two miles south of the south gate of Yellowstone. When first established in 1872, Yellowstone National Park was administered by the U.S. Army. An Army post was located in these meadows.

SOUTH TETON (el. 12,500′) Southern summit of Les Trois Tetons. Not easily visible from the floor of Jackson Hole and cannot be seen from the Teton Park Road because the summit of Nez Perce hides it from view (see Grand Teton).

SPALDING BAY   Southernmost bay on Jackson Lake. Named for Bishop Franklin S. Spalding who made the 1898 ascent of the Grand Teton with W.O. Owen, John Shive, and Frank Petersen.

SPALDING FALLS   Waterfall just below Middle Teton Glacier in Garnet Canyon. Spalding's party passed near these falls on their ascent of the Grand Teton. Named for Bishop Spalding.

SPALDING PEAK (el. 12,029′) First peak west of Cloudveil Dome on the long ridge between Nez Perce and the South Teton. Named for Bishop Spalding (see Spalding Bay).

SPEARHEAD PEAK (el. 10,131′) An imposing fingerlike peak at the head of Death Canyon. There is confusion about the origin of the name. It could be derived from the sharp point of the peak which rises above the flatness of the Fox Creek Divide. It is more likely that the name refers to the spear points and arrowheads which were found in the area. It apparently was a good place for the Indians to hunt mountain sheep.

SPREAD CREEK   Creek channel divides and spreads out on an alluvial fan just before it flows into the Snake River above Triangle X Ranch.

SPRING GULCH   Between the East and West Gros Ventre buttes. Spring Creek flows through this fertile area. Spring Gulch was mentioned in Bradley's report of the 1872 Hayden Expedition.

STATIC PEAK (el. 11,303′) In the Teton Range north of Death Canyon. So named because it is so often hit by lightning.

STEAMBOAT MOUNTAIN (el. 7,872′) At the northern end of Jackson Lake. Peak has an active steam vent.

STEAMBOAT PEAK (el. 10,914′) East of Shoal Lake in the Gros Ventre Range. Its curved, linear shape resembles the prow of a steamboat.

STEWART DRAW   Northwest of Phelps Lake on eastern flank of Teton Range. Named for Henry S.A. Stewart who owned the JY Ranch during the 1920s.

STINKING SPRING   On the old Hoback Canyon Road, east of Hoback Junction emits hydrogen sulfide gas as it flows from an open cave. In 1815 Rev. Samuel Parker recorded that it "emits a frightful stench." Early settlers named it Whoopoop Spring, for obvious reasons. This cold water spring is depositing a bluish white fibrous sulphur.

STORM POINT (el. 10,054′)   On north flank of Cascade Canyon. Companion pinnacle to Ice Point. Receives the brunt of the southwesterly winds.

STRING LAKE   A shallow, narrow lake connecting Leigh and Jenny lakes. Name changed to Beaver Dick Lake in 1931 by approval of USGB in reference to Hayden's guide, Beaver Dick Leigh. However, it appears that String Lake is the older name because it was shown on a Forest Service map from 1928. The name of the lake became established as String again in the 1930s.

SURPRISE LAKE   On the east slope of the Grand Teton, between Garnet Canyon and Glacier Gulch. Earlier called Lake Kinnikinic (an Indian word for a shrub found around the lake), a name evidently suggested by Fritiof Fryxell and approved in 1931 by USGB. The name Surprise Lake was approved in 1938. Its origin is unknown.

SURVEY PEAK (el. 9,277′)   North end of the Teton Range at the west boundary of Grand Teton National Park. This peak may have been climbed in 1877 by a survey party from the 1877 Hayden Expedition. Name appears on the Yellowstone Park Timber Land Reserve Map, 1899.

SWAN LAKE   South of Colter Bay Village. Shallow lake where trumpeter swans and many other waterfowl nest.

SYMMETRY SPIRE (el. 10,500′)   On the north flank of Cascade Canyon. Viewed from the northeast, this small peak is remarkably symmetrical. First ascent by Fritiof Fryxell in 1929, who suggested the name to the Park Service in 1930.

TABLE MOUNTAIN (el. 11,101′)   West of the South Fork of

THIS VIEW OF THE TETON RANGE WAS PHOTOGRAPHED FROM

TABLE MOUNTAIN BY WILLIAM H. JACKSON ON AUGUST 1, 1872.

THIS VIEW, WITH TABLE MOUNTAIN IN THE FOREGROUND,

WAS INCLUDED IN THE SERIES OF ORIGINAL ALBUM PRINTS.

Cascade Canyon. Has a flat top formed by a thin layer of sedimentary rock. The name was selected by the USGS in 1885. In 1872, William H. Jackson ascended Table Mountain from the west, along with an assistant and a mule loaded down with camera, glass plates and all equipment for developing the plates on site, as was necessary at the time. His photographs survive to this day as the first photos of the Tetons.

TAGGART LAKE   At the foot of the Teton Range, north of Beaver Creek. Named for W. Rush Taggart, the assistant geologist with the Hayden expedition of 1872. Taggart had first come to Jackson Hole in 1860 with Captain W.F. Raynolds and the Army Engineers.

LAKE TAMINAH   Just above timberline in Avalanche Canyon. Name comes from a Shoshoni word meaning "spring." Long after summer has come to the valley below, Lake Taminah will still be surrounded by melting snow and spring wildflowers (*see Snowdrift Lake*).

TARGHEE NATIONAL FOREST   Borders Grand Teton National Park on the west. Named for Targhee (sometimes Taghee), a Shoshoni Indian Chief killed by the Crows in 1871.

TEEPE PILLAR   On the east face of the Grand Teton. Named after Theodore Teepee who fell to his death while climbing the Grand Teton in 1925.

TEEWINOT MOUNTAIN (el. 12,325')   Towers above Cascade Canyon and Jenny Lake. Derives its name from the Shoshoni word meaning "many pinnacles." Teewinot probably once applied to the entire Teton Range, rather than just this one peak. Fritiof Fryxell and Phil Smith named the peak when they successfully completed the first ascent of the mountain in 1929.

TERRACE MOUNTAIN (el. 10,258')   In the Teton Wilderness in the Buffalo River, Soda Fork area, a descriptive name for this peak. Name first appeared on the USGS map of 1902.

TETON CANYON   Canyon draining Alaska Basin on the western side of the Range. Thomas Moran ascended it in 1879, for his only visit to the Teton Range.

TETON GLACIER   Between the Grand Teton and Mount Owen. Recent measurements indicate the glacier is moving more rapidly in recent years and may begin to grow in absolute size within another ten to fifteen years.

TETON PASS (el. 8,431')   High mountain pass connecting Victor, Idaho with Wilson, Wyoming. Historically called Hunt's Pass by some, after Wilson Price Hunt. However, it was called Teton Pass by fur trappers in the 1800s.

TETON RANGE   French fur trappers called these mountains *Les Trois Tetons*, meaning the "three breasts." Wilson Price Hunt called them "Pilot Knobs" in 1811 because he had used them for orientation while crossing Union Pass. In his *Journal of a Trapper*, Osborne Russel said that the Shoshoni Indians named the peaks "Hoary Headed Fathers."

TETON VILLAGE   Named in the 1960s as the Jackson Hole Ski Area was developed.

THOR PEAK (el. 12,028')   Southwest of Mount Moran. Named for Thor, the Norse god of thunder.

THOROFARE RIVER   Flows into the Yellowstone River on the Thorofare Plateau in the southeast corner of Yellowstone National Park. This area is a thoroughfare for migrating herds of elk. Indians described it as a place where there is a "passing of great herds."

TIMBERED ISLAND   Southeast of Jenny Lake. A long low "island" of trees practically surrounded by sagebrush. It is a moraine from an early glacier. First appears on a topographic quadrangle map by T.M. Bannon in 1899.

TOGWOTEE PASS (el. 9,650')   Mountain pass west of Moran Junction. Pronounced To-go-tee. In 1873 Captain W.A. Jones of the U.S. Army Engineers named this pass for his Shoshoni Indian guide. The name literally means "lance-thrower" or "lance-striker." Tog-we-tee (from an Indian game of challenge) also means "exactly there." A lance was thrown at a target, then others threw lances to see how close they could come to the first.

TOPPINGS LAKES   West of and below Mount Leidy. Fred Topping, early owner of the Moosehead Ranch, stocked these lakes and took his "dudes" fishing there.

TOSI CREEK, BASIN AND PEAK   Creek is a tributary of the Green River in Bridger National Forest. Named for the Shoshoni Medicine Man who hunted with Owen Wister. The first dude ranch in Wyoming was a hunting lodge built on the creek by William S. Wells in 1897.

TRAVERSE PEAK (el. 11,513') Located on the same ridge as Bivouac Peak. "Traverse" is a skiing and mountaineering term that means to ascend or descend a slope in a diagonal fashion.

TRIPLE GLACIERS Three neighboring glaciers on the northern slope of Mount Moran.

TURPIN MEADOWS East of Moran Junction on the Buffalo River. Dick Turpin came to Jackson Hole to trap in 1887 and died here in 1914. He put up small trapper cabins throughout the area. Turpin Creek, located many miles to the south, is also named after Dick, a testimony to his itinerant lifestyle.

TWO OCEAN LAKE North of Emma Matilda Lake, east of Jackson Lake. Named after Two Ocean Pass many miles to the northeast. Two Ocean is a misnomer for this lake, as its waters drain only into the Pacific.

TWO OCEAN PASS (el. 8,150') In the Teton Wilderness, northeast of Enos Lake. Discovered by Jim Bridger in the early 1830s. Both Atlantic Creek, which eventually drains into the Gulf of Mexico via the Yellowstone and Missouri rivers, and Pacific Creek, which flows down the west slope of the Continental Divide and into the Snake River, have their headwaters on this plateau. Trapper Osborne Russell wrote a description of this divide as he traveled through Thorofare Country in 1835: "We came to a smooth prairie about two miles long, and half a mile wide . . . On the south side of the prairie stands a high snowy peak from whence issues a stream of water which after entering the plain it divides equally one half running West and the other East . . . Here a trout of twelve inches in length may cross the mountains in safety." Thought to be the route that trout took in natural stocking of Yellowstone Lake. Trout couldn't migrate up the Yellowstone River and up over the falls.

UHL HILL (el. 7,443') Southeast of Moran Junction. Named for J.H. Uhl who homesteaded near the hill during the early 1900s.

UPPER SLIDE LAKE Formed by slow-moving, creeping landslides that finally dammed up the Gros Ventre River and

Dr. Seward Webb on the left, and General Coppinger on the right, were leaders of an 1897 expedition to the Teton Mountain Range. Their purpose was to examine the feasibility of the area for National Park status. Webb's dream was not realized until 1929 when this area finally became Grand Teton National Park.

formed the lake in 1916.

VALHALLA CANYON   Between the Grand Teton and Cascade Canyon, running north and south. Named by Jack Durrance and his climbing party who camped here in the shadow of the Grand Teton. They considered this canyon to be the most beautiful in the Teton Range. Great Norse warriors were enshrined in the mythical hall of Valhalla.

WALL, THE (el. 11,050′)   At the head of Avalanche Canyon, a prominent wall of limestone that is a remnant of the layers of sedimentary rock which once overlayed the gneiss, schist, and granite now exposed by the uplifting of the Teton Range.

WALLACE DRAW   North of Mount Leidy near Blackrock Creek. Jim Wallace homesteaded in this area in the early 1900s.

WATERFALLS CANYON   West side of Jackson Lake, north of Moran Bay. Contains Wilderness Falls and Columbine Cascades, two of the most scenic and spectacular waterfalls in Grand Teton National Park.

WEBB CANYON   In the north end of the Teton Range. Named for Dr. Seward Webb who came to Jackson Hole in 1879 on an official expedition led by General Carrington. The expedition scouted the area as a possible national park or perhaps an extension of Yellowstone National Park. Dr. Webb's influence and ideas extended to his son, Vanderbilt Webb, who became John D. Rockefeller's lawyer and president of the Snake River Land Company, which purchased ranch lands in Jackson Hole during the Depression years. Rockefeller subsequently donated these lands to the Park Service and today they are part of the expanded Grand Teton National Park.

WHITEGRASS RANGER STATION   North of Phelps Lake. The ranger cabin and the former dude ranch take their name from the surrounding meadows of grass that turn white after the first frost.

WIGWAMS, THE   When viewed from upper Cascade Canyon, these peaks on the Park's west boundary resemble a row of Indian teepees.

WILCOX POINT   Northwest shore of Jackson Lake. Gale Wilcox, Grand Teton National Park Ranger, lost his life near this point. He was attempting to rescue ranger John Fonda.

The men had broken through the ice while on winter ski patrol. The Valor Award was posthumously conferred upon Wilcox *(see Fonda Point).*

WILDCAT PEAK (el. 9,693′)   Northwest of Lizard Creek. Both cougar and bobcat are still occasionally sighted in this area. YTLR, 1899.

WILLOW FLATS   Northeast of Jackson Lake Dam. A good place to see moose browsing on the many acres of willow bushes.

WILSON   Small village at the foot of the Teton Range, near the southern end of Jackson Hole. Named for its founder Elijah Nicholas "Uncle Nick" Wilson, who in his younger days had been a pony express rider. Living in Utah in 1856, at the age of eleven, Nick was enticed, with the promise of a pinto pony, to go with the Shoshoni. He joined and traveled with Washakie's band, which numbered about 250 Indians at the time. After two years, Nick returned to his family. In 1889, Nick and his brother Sylvester left Utah with their families seeking homesteads and hay for their cattle. In six covered wagons the families made their way over Teton Pass, which had no road at that time. Six years later, in 1895, Nick established the town of Wilson.

WILSON CANYON   East of South Park. Named to honor Uncle Nick's brother, Sylvester. Sylvester Wilson and his family homesteaded in the area now known as South Park. Sylvester Wilson died on 1895 *(see Wilson).*

WIND RIVER LAKE   Just southeast of Togwotee Pass. Named after the Wind River, which heads near the lake. The origin of the river's name is known from "Astoria," Washington Irving's account of the expedition led by Wilson P. Hunt. Hunt's original journal was lost, but Irving's account is accepted as accurate. In 1811 Hunt's Overland Astorians traveled along a stream which Hunt called the Wind River. He reported that the wind blew so constantly in the winter that it prevented snow from accumulating.

WINDY POINT   Scenic turnout along the Teton Park Road just north of Moose. The strong winds here cause deep drifts of snow on the road during winter months.

WISTER, MOUNT (el. 11,490′)   North of Buck Mountain.

UNCLE NICK'S CABIN IN WILSON, WYOMING, IN 1915.

ELIJAH NICHOLAS WILSON WAS ONE OF THE VALLEY'S FIRST

HOMESTEADERS AND FOUNDED THE TOWN OF WILSON IN 1895.

MRS. VILATE SEATON MORRIS ALBUM.

Named to honor the author Owen Wister. His book, The Virginian, which is partially set in Jackson Hole, interested many Easterners in the romance of the West. Wister summered in Jackson Hole and lived to fish and hunt in the surrounding country. Although Fritiof Fryxell submitted the name for this peak in 1931, it was not officially approved until 1939. The Park Service and the USGB have a policy that prohibits naming geographical features for living persons.

WOLVERINE CREEK In the Teton Wilderness, tributary of the upper Snake River. The wolverine, a large, reclusive member of the weasel family, is now so rare that it is rarely seen outside of Alaskan or Canadian wilderness regions. The wolverine is sometimes called the skunk bear because of its apprearance and its foul-smelling scent glands. The creek was named by the Bannon survey in 1899. The wolverine probably once inhabited Jackson Hole in limited numbers and may still be present.

WOODRING, MOUNT (el. 11,590′) South of Mount Moran. Named to honor Samuel Woodring, the first superintendent of Grand Teton National Park. Woodring's varied experience had included work as an army packmaster for General Pershing on the Mexican border; as a guide for Presidents Theodore Roosevelt, Warren Harding, and Calvin Coolidge in Texas and Wyoming; and a career in the National Park Service that began when he went to Yellowstone as a ranger in 1920.

YELLOWSTONE RIVER Called Roche Juane (Yellow Rock) by French fur trappers before 1800. Lewis and Clark were evidently the first Americans to translate and record the name "Yellowstone River." Indians also called the river Mi-tsi-a-dazi, or Yellow Rock River. The name in any language is a reference to the yellowish color of the rhyolite rocks in the Grand Canyon of the Yellowstone River. Rhyolite is igneous rock similar in composition to granite.

YELLOWSTONE POINT (el. 9,783′) Near Yellowstone River in the northern Teton Wilderness. Named after the River. First shown on Owen's Survey Map of Jackson Hole, 1892.

ACKNOWLEDGEMENTS

BETTY HAYDEN AND I COULD NOT HAVE COMPLETED THIS guidebook alone. Without the gracious assistance of Jackson Hole residents, Origins would still be stuck in an anonymous typewriter somewhere between Moose Junction and the Teton County Library.

We would like to acknowledge the assistance of the Teton County Historical Society, especially Dr. Elizabeth Brownell, past president, and the late Dr. Don MacLeod for reviewing the manuscript. Virginia Huidekoper and Erin Muths assisted with the historic photos. Earl Kittleman, Merrill Mattes, Chuck McCurdy, and Patrick Smith reviewed the manuscript and offered technical guidance to this fledgling author. Bob Perkins of the United States Forest Service provided unpaid support which is much appreciated. Sharlene Milligan held all the loose ends together and kept it all on track.

Finally, a most heartfelt thanks to Betty Hayden, my coauthor, who laid the groundwork for the book. She completed many long hours of research, and provided cookies, coffee, and conversation, all of which inspired me to complete the book.

To Betty, who lived a rich, full life and contributed so much to the history of the Park and the Valley.

Cynthia Nielsen

ABOUT THE AUTHORS

ELIZABETH WIED HAYDEN

Elizabeth Wied Hayden, born in 1898 in Waupaka, Wisconsin, first came to the Jackson Hole country in 1927 as a "savage" (seasonal employee of Hamilton stores) in Yellowstone National Park. There she met and married Park Ranger Dudley Hayden in 1929.

A transfer to Grand Teton National Park in 1930 began a long romance with the history of this area. Mrs. Hayden was fascinated by how places and items got their names and traveled extensively gathering information.

The moving force behind the establishment of the Teton County Historical Society, she published her first historical writing, *From Trapper to Tourist in Jackson Hole, in 1957.*

Betty's two sons, Peter and Worth, reflect their early environment. Pete is the Fisheries Biologist in Grand Teton National Park, and Worth is the Director of fisheries for the province of Manitoba in Canada.

Dudley, Grand Teton National Park's second permanent Park Ranger, died in 1969 after a long and active career in the National Park Service and the U.S. Forest Service.

Betty died in 1985 at the age of 87.

CYNTHIA NIELSEN

Cindy Nielsen was first attracted to the mountainous beauty and the unique community of Jackson Hole during a summer job in Yellowstone in 1970. Two years later, she returned to live in the valley and to work as a Park Service ranger-naturalist in Grand Teton National Park. Her work with the National Park Service brought her into contact with many visitors to the valley, and their questions prompted her interest in the origins of Jackson Hole place names.

Cindy left Jackson in 1980 for higher education at the University of Wyoming where she graduated with a Master of Science in Environmental Interpretation. She continues her Park Service career as Chief Naturalist in Channel Islands National Park in Ventura, California. It is her hope that,

"This history of Jackson Hole place names will enliven the travels of valley visitors and the daily lives of Jackson Hole residents. The faces behind the names of these places were those of real and colorful people. Native Americans, fur trappers, early explorers and home-steaders left their unmistakable stamp on Jackson Hole in the names of its lakes, rivers, mountain peaks and high passes."

BIBLIOGRAPHY

Albright, Horace, and Frank Taylor. Oh, Ranger! The Viking Press, Inc. 1972

Bonney, Orin H. and Lorraine G. Bonney's Guide. Houston, Texas 1972.

Fennell, Earle J. A letter written to Mrs. Elizabeth W. Hayden, Jackson, Wyoming, April 10, 1961.

Ferris, Warren A. A letter on file in the Hebard Collection, University of Wyoming, January 10, 1933.

Hayden, Elizabeth Wied. "History of Jackson Hole," Wyoming Geological Association Guidebook, Eleventh Annual Field Conference, 1956.

Hayden, F.V. Sixth Annual Report of the United States Geological Survey. Washington: Government Printing Office, 1879.

Hayden, F.V. Eleventh Annual Report of the United States Geological Survey. Washington: Government Printing Office, 1879.

Irving, Washington. Astoria. New York: G.P. Putnam's Sons Knickerbocker Press. (originally 2 vol. Philadelphia, 1836.)

Linford, Dee. Wyoming Stream Names. Cheyenne, Wyoming: Wyoming Game and Fish Department, 1975.

Mattes, Merrill J. Colter's Hell and Jackson's Hole, Yellowstone Association, 1962.

Mattes, Merrill J. "Jackson Hole, Crossroads of the Western Fur Trade, 1807-1829," Pacific Northwest Quarterly, April, 1946.

Mattes, Merrill J. "Jackson Hole, Crossroads of the Western Fur Trade, 1830-1840," Pacific Northwest Quarterly, January, 1987.

Nelson, Fern. "In the Do-it-yourself Days," Jackson Hole Guide, May 6, 1972, page 2 B.

Parker, Rev. Samuel, Journal of an Exploring Tour. Ithaca, New York: 1842.

Paullin, C. Atlas of the Historical Geography of the United States. Washington, 1932.

Potts, Merlin K., and others. Campfire Tales of Jackson Hole. Grand Teton National History Association, 1970.

Replogle, Wayne F. Yellowstone's Bannock Indian Trails. Yellowstone Association.

Russel, Osborne. Journal of A Trapper. Notes by L.A. York. Boise, Idaho: Syms-York Company, 1921.

Urbanek, Mae. Wyoming Place Names. Third Edition. Boulder, Colorado: Johnson Publishing Company, 1974.

United States Geographic Board, October 5 - November 2, 1927, Washington: Government Printing Office, 5 pages.

Wheat, Carl. Mapping of the Transmississippi West, volumes I, II, III, IV. San Francisco, 1958.

Wilson, E.N. Uncle Nick among the Shoshones. Salt Lake: Skelton Publishers, 1910.

Wright, Gary. "Valley of the Ancients," Teton Magazine, 1975.

THIS PHOTOGRAPH SHOWS THE ENTIRE RANGER CORPS DURING

THE FIRST SUMMER OF PARK OPERATION IN 1929. FIRST PARK

NATURALIST, FRITIOF FRYXELL IS FAR LEFT; SUPERINTENDENT SAM

WOODRING AND MRS. WOODRING ARE IN THE CENTER; RANGER EDWARD

J. BRUCE IS STANDING NEXT TO MRS. WOODRING; AND PHIL SMITH, WHO

HOMESTEADED IN JACKSON HOLE BEFORE GOING TO WORK FOR

GRAND TETON NATIONAL PARK, IS ON THE FAR RIGHT.